CANADIAN *Christmas* COOKING

BY
ROSE MURRAY

McGraw-Hill
Ryerson

Toronto New York Burr Ridge Bangkok Bogotá Caracas
Lisbon London Madrid Mexico City Milan New Delhi
Seoul Singapore Sydney Taipei

First Published in 1979 by James Lorimer & Co.

This edition published 1998 by McGraw-Hill Ryerson Ltd., 300 Water Street, Whitby, Canada, L1N 9B6

2 3 4 5 6 7 8 9 0 W 9 8

Cover design: Matthews Communications Design
Cover photo: Robert Wigington Photography
Illustrations courtesy of Metro Toronto Library

Canadian Cataloguing in Publication Data
Murray, Rose, date
        Canadian Christmas cooking

First published (Lorimer, 1979) under title:
The Christmas cookbook.
ISBN 0-07-551138-X

1. Christmas cookery. 2. Cookery, Canadian.
I. Title. II. Title: Christmas cookbook.

TX739.2.C45M8 1990 641.5'66 C90-095314-4

Printed and bound in Canada
This book was manufactured using acid-free paper.

NOTE:
All ingredients appear in both metric and imperial in the list of ingredients. Pan sizes have been indicated in metric with their imperial counterparts in parentheses. Oven temperatures are indicated throughout in Celsius and Fahrenheit. This double measurement system should eliminate the usual problems of converting.

CONTENTS

DEDICATION

For Allen and Anne, who make my Christmases particularly special.

ACKNOWLEDGEMENTS

I gratefully acknowledge the assistance of the Ontario Arts Council. I wish also to thank the British Columbia Ministry of Agriculture and Food, the Manitoba Department of Agriculture, Manitoba Hydro, the Manitoba Department of Health and Community Services, the Nova Scotia Department of Agriculture and Marketing, the Saskatchewan Department of Agriculture, the Saskatchewan Dairy Foundation, the Quebec Department of Agriculture, Agriculture Canada, the New Brunswick Departments of Agriculture and Fisheries, and the Department of Forestry and Agriculture for Newfoundland and Labrador.

To many individuals, I want to acknowledge special thanks - my husband for his understanding; Monda Rosenberg for her inspiration, encouragement and support; Margaret Fraser for her help with metric conversion; Sandra Hall and Kathryne Durrant for help in metric testing; Lexie Armstrong, Jean and Keith Medley and many, many friends and relatives from Vancouver to Halifax who so willingly gleaned historical material for me, sent me family recipes and gave me much support.

Rose Murray

ABOUT THE AUTHOR

Rose Murray is a well-known food writer, consultant and broadcaster. She has been widely published in magazines and newspapers including Canadian Living, Elm Street and Homemaker's, The Globe & Mail, and The Toronto Star. Rose appears often on a variety of television shows and is resident cook on Kitchener's CKCO-TV Noon News. She acts as a consultant for numerous food companies and government ministries, developing recipes for use in press releases, on packages and in television commercials.

Rose is also the author of New Casseroles and Other One-Dish Meals, Cellar & Silver, Rose Murray's Comfortable Kitchen Cookbook, Rose Murray's Vegetable Cookbook and Secrets of the Sea. She was also a main contributor to over 40 other cookbooks including the popular Canadian Living series.

Rose has studied food and cooking extensively at home and abroad. She has received the Toronto Culinary Guild's Silver Ladle Award for her unique contribution to the food industry. She lives in Cambridge, Ontario, where she writes a weekly column for The Cambridge Reporter.

INTRODUCTION

What would a Canadian Christmas be without custom and tradition? Even in pioneer Canada, when much of settlers' energy was absorbed just surviving the bitter winter, considerable time was devoted to trimming trees, making gifts and preparing a traditional Christmas dinner.

In fact, custom was particularly important when it came to the food for a pioneer Christmas. By baking a plum pudding or stuffing a goose, British settlers could forget, at least for a short time, that they were thousands of miles from their homes and families. For the same reason Ukrainian families would spend weeks preparing the twelve lenten dishes for their Svyata Vechera (holy supper), and Icelandic children would be introduced to the delights of Vinaterta. Familiar Christmas dishes provided both a link to the past and a sense of ethnic identity in a vast, and often harsh, new land.

For early pioneers, finding the necessary ingredients for a traditional favourite was no easy task. Handfuls of scarce luxuries such as sugar, raisins and dried fruits were often hoarded during the fall months in readiness for that one all-important meal, Christmas dinner.

Often substitutions had to be made, and ingenious adaptations of traditional recipes resulted. When ingredients for mincemeat were scarce, for instance, apples from the cold cellar and carrots were used instead to make an unusual and delicious Winter Pie. In time a combination of adapted recipes and traditional ethnic favourites came to form a distinctive Canadian cuisine for the Christmas season.

This new Christmas tradition in food was further enriched as recipes were exchanged between friends and neighbours of different ethnic backgrounds. The custom of baking elaborate Christmas cookies, for example, was brought to Canada by settlers of German origin and soon became popular in homes across the country.

Today Canadian Christmas cooking bears the stamp of the rich and varied Canadian tradition which has emerged since the first settlers came to this country. The recipes collected in this book pay tribute to that tradition. They were gathered from family collections from all across the country and represent both traditional ethnic favourites as well as some of the unique and delicious adaptations which originated in early Canadian homes. The menus at the end of the book were designed to help those interested to prepare a holiday feast which reflects a wide range of ethnic favourites. Try the recipes from other cultures as well as your old stand-bys. It is this kind of exchange that will enrich an already cherished holiday.

CAKES

INTRODUCTION

The custom of having cakes and other sweets at Christmas originated in England, when cakes were given to the poor women who sang carols in the streets. British settlers introduced fruit cakes to Canada, and settlers from other countries brought their traditional Christmas recipes with them, too. On Christmas Eve in Nova Scotia, for instance, village people would participate in the Dutch and German custom of "Bell Snicklers." Dressed in traditional costumes, they would call on their neighbours, announcing the holiday season with bells and horns and wishing all "Merry Christmas and Happy New Year." The callers would then be invited in for singing and Christmas cakes with wine. And in Newfoundland, the mummers, a troupe of professional entertainers, served cake and drinks at each village on their holiday season tour.

In Canada today, Christmas is almost the only time of year when these special cakes are made. (Wedding feasts are another time, and some of the larger fruit cakes in this chapter would be perfect for a wedding cake.)

Most people have personal favourites, often recipes which have been passed down from mother to daughter through the generations. The cakes in this chapter have been adapted from cherished family collections from all parts of the country. They represent a variety of cultural traditions—from British to Swedish and Ukrainian—and they range in taste and size to accommodate a variety of personal preferences.

Preparing Christmas cakes is a labour of love in Canadian homes. Here are some tips which will help make that labour enjoyable and the results well worth the effort.

The Ingredients

For a truly successful cake, use only fresh ingredients. All of the recipes in this chapter were prepared with large eggs, and where butter is indicated, sweet or unsalted butter may be used.

Cake Pans

Loaf tins have been suggested for most of the recipes which follow because they are standard equipment in most kitchens. Other pans or tins may be used instead, but the baking time should be adjusted according to the pan size.

Baking the Cake

A shallow pan of hot water placed in the oven while the cake bakes will help to keep the cake moist. If the top of the cake appears to be drying out, simply place a double layer of ungreased brown paper over the top.

Testing for Doneness

Baking time varies according to the pan size, the richness of the batter and the oven. To avoid over-baking the cake, test it with a skewer at least one half hour before the recommended time. Insert the skewer into the middle of the cake, but remember that it may be sticky because of the fruit. However it should not be gummy with batter.

Storing the Cake

Most cakes become moist and mellow and improve in flavour if they are baked a few weeks before they are to be served. Storing is an important factor in the success of the cake.

For best results, let the cake cool completely after it has come out of the oven. Make several holes through the cake with a skewer and pour in heated (but not boiled) brandy. Moisten cheesecloth with sherry or brandy (not table wine) and wrap it around the cake. Finally wrap the cake in foil and store it in a tightly covered tin in a cool place.

Although there is no need to refrigerate a fruit cake, it should be checked periodically to insure that it hasn't become too moist or too dry. If it is too moist, there is a danger of moulding. To avoid this, let the cake air for a while. If the cake becomes dry, moisten the cheesecloth again with sherry or brandy.

Cakes will keep for months, sometimes years, if they are stored properly.

WHITE COCOANUT-FRUIT CAKE

This small white fruit cake has been one of my favourites for years. It is very moist and filled with fruit and nuts.

750	mL diced mixed candied fruit	(3 cups)
375	mL halved red and green candied cherries	(1½ cups)
375	mL diced candied pineapple	(1½ cups)
750	mL light seedless raisins	(3 cups)
250	mL desiccated cocoanut	(1 cup)
250	mL blanched slivered almonds	(1 cup)
500	mL all-purpose flour	(2 cups)
10	mL baking powder	(2 tsp)
2	mL salt	(½ tsp)
125	mL butter	(½ cup)
250	mL granulated sugar	(1 cup)
3	eggs	
5	mL almond extract	(1 tsp)
75	mL orange juice	(¼ cup)
50	mL brandy	(¼ cup)

Prepare two 2 L (9"x 5") loaf tins by greasing them with butter and lining them with buttered brown paper. Preheat the oven to 120°C (250°F).

Combine all the fruit and nuts in a large bowl and dredge them with 50 mL (¼ cup) of the flour. Sift the remaining flour together with the baking powder and salt.

In a large bowl, cream the butter, add the granulated sugar and beat until light and fluffy. Add the eggs, one at a time, beating well after each addition. Add the almond extract.

Stir in the orange juice and brandy alternately with the sifted dry ingredients.

Fold in the floured fruit and nuts. Turn into the prepared pans and bake for 3 hours, or until a skewer inserted in the middle of each cake comes out clean. Cool for 30 minutes in the pans, then turn out onto racks. Carefully remove the paper and cool completely. Yields 2.5 kg (5 lbs) cake.

LIGHT BRAZIL NUT FRUIT CAKE

Crammed full of fruit and whole Brazil nuts, this large moist fruit cake not only makes a beautiful Christmas cake, but is also perfect as a wedding cake.

Make sure the Brazil nuts are very fresh; rancid ones will spoil the taste of your cake.

125	mL all-purpose flour	(½ cup)
1.5	L light seedless raisins	(6 cups)
750	mL red candied cherries	(3 cups)
750	mL green candied cherries	(3 cups)
750	mL diced mixed candied fruit	(3 cups)
1	L whole Brazil nuts	(4 cups)
500	mL butter	(2 cups)
500	mL granulated sugar	(2 cups)
12	eggs, separated	
15	mL almond extract	(1 Tbs)
1	L all-purpose flour	(4 cups)
10	mL baking powder	(2 tsp)
2	mL salt	(½ tsp)
500	mL crushed pineapple, undrained	(2 cups)

Cut the cherries into halves or quarters, then dredge the raisins, candied fruit and nuts in the 125 mL flour. Let this mixture sit overnight so that the flavours will mingle.

Prepare four 2 L (9" x 5") loaf tins (or other fruit cake tins as desired) by greasing them with butter and lining them with buttered brown paper. Preheat the oven to 120°C (250°F).

Cream the butter thoroughly and add the sugar gradually, beating until light and fluffy.

Beat the egg whites until stiff, but still moist. Set aside.

Beat the egg yolks and add them to the creamed mixture. Stir in the almond extract.

Sift together the 1 L flour, baking powder and salt. Add the dry ingredients to the creamed mixture a bit at a time, stirring only to blend after each addition. Mix in the crushed pineapple and pineapple juice and stir in the prepared fruit. Fold in the stiff egg whites.

Turn the batter into the prepared pans and bake for about 3½ hours, or until a skewer inserted in the middle of each cake comes out clean. Cool for 30 minutes in the pans, then turn out onto racks. Carefully remove the paper and cool completely. Use the almond paste and icing recipes at the end of this chapter to decorate the cakes before serving. Yields 5 kg (10 lbs) cake.

RICH LIGHT FRUIT CAKE

The distinctive taste of ginger and the rich flavour of pecans give this medium-light fruit cake a special appeal.

125	mL granulated sugar	(½ cup)
250	mL water	(1 cup)
15	mL corn syrup	(1 Tbs)
750	mL white seedless raisins	(3 cups)
750	mL chopped red candied cherries	(3 cups)
750	mL chopped green candied cherries	(3 cups)
125	mL diced candied lemon peel	(½ cup)
250	mL diced candied orange peel	(1 cup)
575	mL diced candied citron peel	(2⅓ cups)
650	mL chopped candied pineapple	(2⅔ cups)
175	mL chopped candied ginger	(¾ cup or 6 oz jar)
550	mL blanched almond halves	(2¼ cups)
1	L pecan halves	(4 cups)
250	mL brandy	(1 cup)
500	mL butter	(2 cups)
1	L all-purpose flour	(4 cups)
8	eggs	
625	mL granulated sugar	(2½ cups)

Make a syrup by boiling the 125 mL granulated sugar and water together for 5 minutes. Add the corn syrup and set aside.

Place the fruit and nuts in a large glass bowl. Add 125 mL (½ cup) of the syrup and all of the brandy. Stir to mix thoroughly, cover tightly and let sit for 24 hours. Stir occasionally.

When you are ready to bake the cake, prepare four 2 L (9" x 5") loaf tins or other pans of your choice. Grease the pans with butter and line them with buttered brown paper. Preheat the oven to 120°C (250°F).

To prepare the batter, cream the butter well. Add the flour gradually, creaming to blend smoothly. In another bowl, beat the eggs lightly and gradually beat in the 625 mL sugar. Stir the two mixtures together until smooth. Stir only to blend. Add the fruit and nuts gradually, folding and mixing together gently with your hands.

Turn into the prepared pans and bake for about 4 hours, or until a skewer inserted in the middle of each cake comes out clean.

Cool for 30 minutes in the pans, then turn out onto racks. Carefully remove the paper and cool completely. Although this cake is moist and delicious after a few days, let it ripen 3 to 4 weeks for best results. Use the almond paste and icing recipes at the end of this chapter to decorate the cake before serving.

Yields 5 kg (10 lbs) cake.

Note: Since there is no baking powder or baking soda in this cake, the texture will be somewhat dense.

DUNDEE CAKE

This white Scottish fruit cake was well known to many early Canadian settlers. It is a delicate cake with just a smattering of fruit.

625	mL all-purpose flour	(2½ cups)
5	mL baking powder	(1 tsp)
2	mL salt	(½ tsp)
150	mL chopped maraschino cherries	(⅔ cup)
250	mL seedless light raisins	(1 cup)
325	mL currants	(1⅓ cups)

250 mL butter	(1 cup minus 2 Tbs)
150 mL granulated sugar	(⅔ cup)
4 eggs	
15 mL lemon juice	(1 Tbs)
2 mL almond extract	(½ tsp)

Prepare a 2 L (9"x5") loaf tin by greasing it with butter and lining it with buttered brown paper. Preheat the oven to 140°C (275°F).

Sift together the flour, baking powder and salt.

Drain the cherries thoroughly in a sieve and then on a paper towel. Combine them with the raisins and currants and dredge the fruit with 50mL (¼ cup) of the dry ingredients.

Cream the butter, add the sugar and beat until light and fluffy. Add the eggs, one at a time, beating well after each addition. Stir in the lemon juice and almond extract.

Gradually stir the dry ingredients into the creamed mixture, mixing only to blend. Stir in the prepared fruit.

Turn into the prepared pan and bake for 2 hours, or until a skewer inserted in the middle of the cake comes out clean.

Cool for 20 minutes in the pan, then turn out onto a rack. Carefully remove the paper and cool completely. Use the almond paste and icing recipes at the end of this chapter to decorate the cake before serving.
Yields 2 kg (4 lbs) cake.

CHERRY CAKE

The almonds and cocoanut in this cake give it an unusual crunchy texture. Cherry Cake is small and light, not heavily loaded with fruit.

125 mL butter	(½ cup)
250 mL granulated sugar	(1 cup)
3 eggs, separated	
5 mL cherry extract	(1 tsp)

425 mL all-purpose flour	(1¾ cups)
5 mL baking powder	(1 tsp)
1 mL salt	(¼ tsp)
50 mL milk	(¼ cup)
300 mL chopped blanched almonds	(1¼ cups)
50 mL shredded cocoanut	(¼ cup)
75 mL citron	(⅓ cup)
175 mL whole candied cherries	(¾ cup)

Prepare a 2 L (9"x5") loaf tin by buttering it and lining with buttered brown paper. Preheat the oven to 140°C (275°F).

Cream the butter, add the sugar gradually and beat until light and fluffy. Beat the egg yolks well and add to the creamed mixture. Stir in the cherry extract. Use 50 mL (¼ cup) of the flour to dredge the fruit and nuts.

Sift the remaining flour with the baking powder and salt. Slowly add the dry ingredients, alternately with the milk, to the creamed mixture. Stir in the prepared fruit and nuts. Beat the egg whites until stiff, but still moist, and carefully fold them into the batter. The batter should be quite stiff. Turn into the prepared pan.

Bake for about 3 hours, or until a skewer inserted in the middle of the cake comes out clean.

Cool for 20 minutes in the pan, then turn out onto a rack. Carefully remove the paper and cool completely. Use the almond paste and icing recipes at the end of this chapter to decorate the cake before serving.
Yields 1 kg (2½ lbs) cake.

SPICY APRICOT-PECAN FRUIT CAKE

Medium in size and colour, this spicy fruit cake has a more "cakey" texture than some of the others in this chapter.

150	mL chopped candied pineapple	(⅔ cup)
250	mL chopped dried apricots	(1 cup)
1	L large seeded raisins	(4 cups)
500	mL currants	(2 cups)
375	mL golden sultana raisins	(1½ cups)
375	mL diced mixed peel	(1½ cups)
175	mL diced candied cherries	(¾ cup)
250	mL chopped pecans	(1 cup)
375	mL granulated sugar	(1½ cups)
375	mL apricot nectar	(1½ cups)
250	mL butter	(1 cup)
3	eggs	
625	mL all-purpose flour	(2½ cups)
5	mL baking powder	(1 tsp)
5	mL baking soda	(1 tsp)
2	mL salt	(½ tsp)
5	mL cinnamon	(1 tsp)
5	mL ground allspice	(1 tsp)
5	mL mace	(1 tsp)

In a large heavy pan, boil together all the fruit, nuts, sugar and apricot nectar, stirring constantly for 5 minutes. Remove from the heat, add the butter and stir well. Cool. The flavours will mingle more if this mixture is allowed to sit overnight.

The batter for this cake will fill two 2 L (9" x 5") loaf pans, plus a small can suitable for gift-giving. Prepare the pans by greasing them with butter and lining them with buttered brown paper. Preheat the oven to 150°C (300°F).

Beat the eggs thoroughly and add them to the fruit mixture.

Sift together the flour, baking powder, baking soda, salt and spices. Add the dry ingredients to the fruit and egg mixture and stir well to combine. Turn into the prepared pans, leaving room for the batter to expand.

Bake the cakes in loaf tins for 2 to 2½ hours; bake the small can for 30 minutes to 45 minutes, or until a skewer inserted in the middle of the cake comes out clean.

Cool the cakes in the pans for 30 minutes, then turn out onto racks. Carefully remove the paper and cool completely. Use the almond paste and icing recipes at the end of this chapter to decorate the cakes before serving.

Yields 3 kg (6 lbs) cake.

DARK RUM NUT FRUIT CAKE

Soaking the fruit and nuts overnight allows the flavours of this moist, fruit-laden cake to mingle.

1.5	L diced mixed candied peel	(6 cups)
1.5	L seedless dark raisins	(6 cups)
1	L currants	(4 cups)
375	mL diced candied citron	(1½ cups)
375	mL halved red candied cherries	(1½ cups)
375	mL halved green candied cherries	(1½ cups)
500	mL blanched slivered almonds	(2 cups)
500	mL coarsely chopped walnuts	(2 cups)
250	mL dark rum	(1 cup)
125	mL all-purpose flour	(½ cup)
500	mL butter	(2 cups)
625	mL lightly packed brown sugar	(2½ cups)
7	eggs	
15	mL vanilla	(1 Tbs)
750	mL all-purpose flour	(3 cups)
10	mL baking powder	(2 tsp)
2	mL salt	(½ tsp)
10	mL cinnamon	(2 tsp)
5	mL ground cloves	(1 tsp)

In a large bowl, combine the fruit and nuts. Pour the rum over the fruit and mix thoroughly. Cover and let sit overnight.

Prepare four 2 L (9" x 5") loaf tins (or other fruit cake tins as desired) by buttering them and lining them with buttered brown paper. Preheat the oven to 120°C (250°F).

Drain any liquid from the fruit and set it aside. Dredge the fruit with the 125 mL flour.

Cream the butter, add the brown sugar and beat until light and fluffy. Add the eggs, one at a time, beating thoroughly after each addition. Add the vanilla and reserved liquid from the fruit.

Sift together the 750 mL flour, baking powder, salt, cinnamon and cloves. Add gradually to creamed mixture, stirring just to blend. Stir in the floured fruit and nuts.

Turn into the prepared pans and bake for 3 to 3½ hours, or until a skewer inserted in the middle of each cake comes out clean. Cool for 30 minutes in the pans, then turn out onto racks. Carefully remove the paper and cool completely.Use the almond paste and icing recipes at the end of this chapter to decorate the cakes before serving.

Yields 5 kg (10 lbs) cake.

BANANA FRUIT CAKE

A very moist cake with a rich spicy flavour, Banana Fruit Cake will ripen completely within two weeks. In fact, the flavour and texture are good the day it is baked.

750	mL chopped mixed candied fruit	(3 cups)
500	mL chopped pitted dates	(2 cups)
125	mL chopped candied pineapple	(½ cup)
250	mL chopped walnuts	(1 cup)
625	mL all-purpose flour	(2½ cups)
5	mL baking powder	(1 tsp)
5	mL baking soda	(1 tsp)
5	mL salt	(1 tsp)
5	mL cinnamon	(1 tsp)
1	mL freshly grated nutmeg	(¼ tsp)
1	mL ground cloves	(¼ tsp)
200	mL soft butter	(¾ cup)
500	mL lightly packed brown sugar	(2 cups)
4	eggs	
5	mL grated orange rind	(1 tsp)
15	mL orange juice	(1 Tbs)
2	mL orange extract	(½ tsp)
375	mL mashed ripe bananas	(1½ cups)

Prepare two 2 L (9" x 5") loaf tins by greasing them with butter and lining them with buttered brown paper. Preheat the oven to 150°C (300°F).

In a large bowl combine the fruit, dates, pineapple and walnuts. Dredge them with 50 mL (¼ cup) of the flour. Sift the remaining flour together with the baking powder, baking soda, salt, cinnamon, nutmeg and cloves. Set aside.

Cream the butter, add the sugar and beat until the mixture is light and fluffy. Beat in the eggs, one at a time. Beat in the orange rind, orange juice and orange extract.

Mash the bananas with a fork. (A food processor will tend to liquefy the bananas and this will change the texture of the cake.) Alternately stir the bananas and the flour mixture into the creamed mixture. Stir in the floured fruit and nuts.

Turn into the prepared pans and bake for 2 hours and 15 minutes, or until a skewer inserted in the middle of each cake comes out clean.

Cool in the pans for 20 minutes, then turn out onto racks. Carefully remove the paper and allow the cakes to cool completely. Yields 2 loaf cakes or about 2 kg (5 lbs).

CRANBERRY-GLAZED CHEESECAKE

Crust

250 mL all-purpose flour	(1 cup)
50 mL granulated sugar	(¼ cup)
5 mL grated lemon rind	(1 tsp)
1 egg yolk	
2 mL vanilla	(½ tsp)
50 mL softened butter	(¼ cup)

Filling

5 eggs, separated	
50 mL granulated sugar	(¼ cup)
450 g cream cheese	(1 lb)
150 mL granulated sugar	(⅔ cup)
15 mL grated lemon rind	(1 Tbs)
45 mL lemon juice	(3 Tbs)
50 mL all-purpose flour	(¼ cup)
5 mL vanilla	(1 tsp)
250 mL sour cream	(1 cup)

Topping

175 mL granulated sugar	(¾ cup)
1 envelope unflavoured gelatin	
175 mL water	(¾ cup)
500 mL cranberries	(2 cups)
5 mL grated lemon rind	(1 tsp)
30 mL lemon juice	(2 Tbs)

Lightly grease a 3 L (9") springform pan. Preheat the oven to 160°C (325°F).

To make the crust, combine the flour, sugar and lemon rind. Make a well in the centre of the dry ingredients and in it place the egg yolk, vanilla and butter. Blend with a fork, then mix with your fingers until the dough starts to hold together. It will be fairly crumbly. Press evenly on the bottom and sides of the prepared pan. (The dough won't cover all of the sides.)

To prepare the filling, beat the egg whites into stiff but moist peaks. Gradually beat in the 50 mL granulated sugar. Beat until stiff and shiny. Set aside.

Cream the cream cheese until softened. Beat in the egg yolks, one at a time. Gradually beat in the 150 mL sugar, lemon rind, lemon juice, flour, vanilla and sour cream. Fold in the stiff egg whites.

Pour into the prepared crust. Bake for 1¼ hours, or until almost set. Cool for 10 minutes. Run a spatula carefully around the edge to loosen, then cool thoroughly.

To prepare the topping, combine the sugar and gelatin in a saucepan. Gradually add the water. Slowly bring to a boil, stirring often. Add the cranberries, lemon rind and juice. Cook, stirring, for about 5 minutes, until the skins pop.

Refrigerate until the cooling mixture begins to thicken, stirring occasionally.

With a spatula, loosen the pan sides from the cool cheesecake and remove them. Loosen the cheesecake from the bottom of the pan with a spatula and carefully slide the cheesecake onto a serving plate.

Pour the cranberry mixture onto the cheesecake, spreading it over the top. Refrigerate for about 3 hours, until topping is set. If the cheesecake has been refrigerated for longer, remove it from the refrigerator 45 minutes to 1 hour before serving for a creamier texture.

Yields 12 servings.

BLACK BUN

This Scottish fruit cake enclosed in pastry is probably less familiar to Canadians than Dundee Cake. Although it is traditionally served on New Year's Eve, Black Bun is an interesting and attractive cake to have on hand all through the holiday season.

Pastry

625	mL all-purpose flour	(2½ cups)
3	mL baking powder	(¾ tsp)
250	mL chilled butter	(1 cup)
90-120	mL ice water	(6-8 Tbs)

Filling

1	L all-purpose flour	(4 cups)
5	mL baking soda	(1 tsp)
1	mL salt	(¼ tsp)
5	mL cinnamon	(1 tsp)
5	mL ground ginger	(1 tsp)
2	mL freshly ground black pepper	(½ tsp)
1	mL ground cloves	(¼ tsp)
1.5	L seedless raisins	(6 cups)
500	mL seeded raisins	(2 cups)
875	mL currants	(3½ cups)
250	mL diced mixed candied peel	(1 cup)
250	mL blanched slivered almonds	(1 cup)
2	eggs	
250	mL lightly packed brown sugar	(1 cup)
250	mL sour milk or buttermilk	(1 cup)
125	mL brandy	(½ cup)
1	egg, slightly beaten	

To prepare the pastry, combine the flour and baking powder. Cut the butter into tiny pieces and rub it into the flour until it resembles coarse rolled oats. Be sure that your hands are not too warm when doing this and work as quickly as possible. Pour in 90 mL of ice water. Shape the dough into a ball. Do not overwork it. If it crumbles too much, add more ice water by the spoonful. Wrap and chill the dough for 1 to 2 hours.

Butter the bottom and sides of a round cake tin 20 cm (8") in diameter and 7.5 cm (3") high. Preheat the oven to 180°C (350°F).

Break off two-thirds of the chilled pastry. On a lightly floured board roll it out into a circle approximately 40 cm (16") in diameter and 6 mm (N") thick. Gently press the pastry into the prepared pan, being careful not to stretch it. Trim off the excess dough, leaving a tiny rim of it all around the tin. Roll the remaining pastry into a 25 cm (10") circle and set aside for the top.

Prepare the filling by sifting the flour, baking soda, salt, cinnamon, ginger, pepper and cloves into a large bowl. Add the raisins, currants, peel and almonds. Mix well to coat with flour.

Beat the eggs, add the brown sugar and beat well together. Stir in the milk and brandy. Mix together with the flour and fruit mixture and combine everything well. Spoon into the pastry-lined tin. Cover with the pastry top. Do not stretch. Seal tightly to the tiny rim of pastry around the tin and crimp slightly with your fingers or the tines of a fork. With a fork, prick the pastry all over the top, and cut two small slits in the centre with a sharp knife. Brush the top with beaten egg.

Bake at 180°C (350°F) for 1½ hours. Reduce the heat to 140°C (275°F) and bake for another 1½ hours, or until the top is golden brown. Cool completely in tin, then carefully remove and cover tightly with foil. Let sit at room temperature for a week before serving. Black Bun keeps for 3 to 4 weeks and will freeze well.

Yields 3 kg (6½ lbs) cake.

OLD-FASHIONED POUND CAKE

Pound Cake was so named because all of the ingredients weighed one pound each–butter, sugar, eggs and flour. In some early households, particularly in the Maritimes, there always had to be a Pound Cake at Christmas.

It was said that the cake was best if made by two people–one to beat the sugar and butter, the other to sift the flour and beat the eggs. This co-operative effort by neighbours was quite practical because the more the Pound Cake was beaten, the finer the texture, and the lighter the cake, since no baking powder or baking soda was used to help it rise.

Like early recipes, this Pound Cake is made without any leavening. An electric mixer will incorporate air into the batter if no helpful neighbour is available.

250	mL butter	(1 cup)
250	mL granulated sugar	(1 cup)
5	eggs, separated	
10	mL grated lemon rind	(2 tsp)
25	mL lemon juice	(1½ Tbs)
5	mL vanilla	(1 tsp)
15	mL brandy	(1 Tbs)
550	mL all-purpose flour	(2¼ cups)

Prepare a 2 L (9″ x 5″) loaf tin by greasing it with butter and lining it with buttered wax paper. Preheat the oven to 160°C (325°F).

Using an electric mixer cream the butter until very smooth. Gradually add the sugar, beating well until very light and fluffy.

With an electric mixer, beat the egg yolks until light-coloured and creamy and add to them the grated rind, lemon juice, vanilla and brandy. Beat this mixture well into the butter and sugar mixture. Very gradually stir in the flour.

Beat the egg whites until they are stiff , but not dry. Fold them into the batter, a third at a time.

Spoon into the prepared tin and bake for 1 hour and 20 minutes, or until light golden brown, and a skewer inserted in the middle of the cake comes out clean. Cool in the pan for 10 minutes, then turn out onto a rack. Carefully remove the wax paper and cool completely.

The cake keeps well wrapped in a brandy-soaked cheesecloth in a tin. It does not freeze well.

Yields 1 loaf cake.

BÛCHE DE NOËL

(Yule Log)

A traditional French holiday cake, the Christmas Log is made and decorated to resemble the yule-log, the burning of which means friendliness and warmth. It is often served in French-Canadian homes as a spectacular ending for the Christmas Eve dinner.

Cake

250	mL cake and pastry flour	(1 cup)
300	mL granulated sugar	(1¼ cups)
4	eggs, separated	
1	mL salt	(¼ tsp)
5	mL vanilla	(1 tsp)
	icing sugar	

Rum Syrup

50	mL granulated sugar	(¼ cup)
50	mL water	(¼ cup)
15	mL dark rum	(1 Tbs)

Coffee Cream

150	mL granulated sugar	(⅔ cup)
125	mL water	(½ cup)
3	egg yolks	
250	mL soft butter	(1 cup)
15	mL very strong coffee	(1 Tbs)
20	mL dark rum	(1½ Tbs)

Chocolate Butter Icing

50	mL soft butter	(¼ cup)
500	mL sifted icing sugar	(2 cups)
30	mL cream	(2 Tbs)
	pinch of salt	
2	mL vanilla	(½ tsp)

2	squares unsweetened chocolate, melted	(2 oz)
	candied cherries and candied citron or angelica	

To make the cake, grease a 2 L (10½" x 15½") jelly-roll pan with butter, line with buttered wax paper and sprinkle with flour. Preheat the oven to 200°C (400°F).

Sift together the flour and 250 ml (1 cup) of the sugar. Beat the egg whites with the salt until stiff. Gradually beat in the remaining 50 mL (¼ cup) sugar.

Beat the egg yolks until thick. Beat in the vanilla. Fold in the stiffly beaten egg whites. Then fold in the flour mixture very gradually, a bit at a time.

Turn the batter into the prepared pan and spread it evenly. Bake for 15 minutes, or until the cake springs back when lightly pressed.

Sprinkle a clean tea towel with icing sugar. Turn the hot cake out onto the towel and remove the pan and lining carefully. Trim off any hard edges. Roll the cake and towel up from long side and cool. The roll should be long and thin.

Meanwhile, prepare the rum syrup by boiling the sugar and water together for about 3 minutes, or until syrupy. The syrup will burn if cooked too long, so watch it carefully as it cooks. Cool and add the rum.

To prepare the coffee cream, boil together the sugar and water until the mixture reaches the soft ball stage (115°C or 240°F). Beat the egg yolks until thick. Beat the hot syrup gradually into the egg yolks and continue beating until the mixture is lukewarm. Add the butter, bit by bit, still beating constantly. Beat in the coffee and rum. Let cool completely and chill briefly if too runny.

Unroll the cake and brush it with half the rum syrup. Spread on the coffee cream, reserving 50 mL (¼ cup) for later. Roll up the cake like a jelly roll. Wrap it in wax paper and chill until the cream is firm.

To prepare the chocolate butter icing, cream the butter, add about half the icing sugar and beat until fluffy. Add the salt and vanilla. Stir in the remaining sugar alternately with the cream. Blend in the chocolate. Beat until the icing stands in sharp peaks. If the icing is too stiff, add a bit more cream.

Remove the wax paper from the rolled cake. Cut a small roll from each end of the cake diagonally with a knife. These rolls will serve as knots. Brush the outside of the cake and the knots with the rest of the rum syrup. Attach the knots (the rum syrup will act as a glue). Using the reserved coffee cream, decorate the ends of the knots and the ends of the log.

Spread the rest of the cake with the prepared chocolate butter icing. Using a pastry tube filled with the icing, decorate the log and knots to look like bark, or apply icing smoothly over the entire log and run a fork along the length of the log.

Decorate the finished log with candied cherries and angelica or candied citron cut to resemble holly leaves.

Store the finished cake in a cool place until serving time so that the coffee cream icing does not become too soft. If you store it in the refrigerator, let the cake return to room temperature before serving.
Yields 10 to 12 servings.

SOUR CREAM COFFEE CAKE

Topping

75	mL butter	(⅓ cup)
250	mL icing sugar	(1 cup)
125	mL all-purpose flour	(½ cup)
15	mL cinnamon	(2½ tsp)
5	mL grated orange rind	(1 tsp)
5	mL grated lemon rind	(1 tsp)
125	mL finely chopped pecans or walnuts	(½ cup)

Batter

125	mL butter	(½ cup)
250	mL granulated sugar	(1 cup)
2	eggs	
5	mL vanilla	(1 tsp)
500	mL all-purpose flour	(2 cups)
5	mL baking powder	(1 tsp)
1	mL salt	(¼ tsp)
5	mL baking soda	(1 tsp)
250	mL sour cream	(1 cup)

Grease a 3.5 L (9" x 13") pan. Preheat the oven to 180°C (350°F).

To prepare the topping, cream the butter and icing sugar. Add the flour, cinnamon, rind and nuts. It's not necessary for this mixture to be smooth. Set aside.

To prepare the batter, cream the butter, add the granulated sugar and beat until light and fluffy. Beat in the eggs, one at a time, then the vanilla.

Sift together the flour, baking powder and salt. Mix the baking soda with the sour cream. Stir half of the dry ingredients into the creamed mixture. Add the sour cream, then stir in the remaining dry ingredients.

Spread in the prepared pan. Sprinkle on the topping and bake for 35 minutes, or until a skewer inserted in the middle of the cake comes out clean. Serve warm.

Sour Cream Coffee Cake freezes well. To reheat the cake, wrap it tightly in foil and heat it for 20 minutes in a 180°C (350°F) oven.
Yields 10 to 12 servings.

VINATERTA

Vinaterta is an Icelandic Christmas torte that improves with age. Although it is dry at first, it will become moist and flavourful if left, well covered, for at least a week. This particular version is from an Icelandic community in Saskatchewan.

125 mL shortening	(½ cup)
125 mL butter	(½ cup)
375 mL granulated sugar	(1½ cups)
3 eggs	
45 mL cream	(3 Tbs)
15 mL almond extract	(1 Tbs)
875 mL cake and pastry flour	(3½ cups)
15 mL baking powder	(1 Tbs)
5 mL ground cardamom	(1 tsp)

Filling

500 g chopped dates	(1 lb)
175 mL granulated sugar	(¾ cup)
125 mL water	(½ cup)
5 mL vanilla	(1 tsp)
15 mL lemon juice	(1 Tbs)

Icing

30 mL butter	(2 Tbs)
250 mL icing sugar	(1 cup)
2 mL almond extract	(½ tsp)
45 mL hot water	(3 Tbs)

Grease and flour six 1.5 L (9") round cake pans. (If you do not have six pans, bake your cake in a couple of batches.) Preheat the oven to 190°C (375°F).

Cream the shortening, butter and sugar until light and fluffy. Add the eggs, one at a time, beating well after each addition.

Stir in the cream and almond extract. Sift the flour, baking powder and cardamom together and add to the creamed mixture. The batter will be very stiff.

Divide batter into six equal parts and pat each part into a prepared pan. Since the batter is so stiff, it will be difficult to spread. If worked in a circular motion, it will stay in place. Make sure it is as even as possible in pans.

Bake the layers for 12 to 15 minutes, or until golden brown. Remove from the pans and cool flat on racks. When cool, stack the layers on top of each other with filling between each layer.

To prepare the filling, combine the dates, sugar and water in a saucepan. Cook over low heat for about 5 minutes, until smooth and thick. Remove from the heat. Add the vanilla and lemon juice and cool. Spread evenly between the layers of cake.

To prepare the icing, cream together the butter and icing sugar. Stir in the almond extract and hot water to make a smooth thin icing. Pour and spread over the top layer, letting it drip down sides of cake. Serve the torte in very thin slices.

Yields twenty-four 2 cm (1") servings.

Prune Variation:
Substitute 500 g (1 lb) prunes for the dates in the filling, or use half prunes and half dates. The more traditional filling is the prune one, but dates are especially good.

CHRISTMAS MEDIVNYK
(Ukrainian Honey Cake)

Cakes and pastries made with honey are a tradition at the Ukrainian Christmas Eve supper or "Svyata Vechera." Prairie buckwheat honey gives a very rich colour and flavour to these desserts.

250	mL honey	(1 cup)
125	mL butter	(½ cup)
250	mL lightly packed brown sugar	(1 cup)
4	eggs, separated	
750	mL all-purpose flour	(3 cups)
5	mL baking powder	(1 tsp)
1	mL salt	(¼ tsp)
5	mL cinnamon	(1 tsp)
2	mL ground cloves	(½ tsp)
1	mL freshly grated nutmeg	(¼ tsp)
10	mL baking soda	(2 tsp)
250	mL sour cream	(1 cup)
250	mL chopped walnuts	(1 cup)
	icing sugar	
	whipped cream	

Butter a 3 L (10") tube pan. Preheat the oven to 160°C (325°F).

Bring the honey to a boil, then let it cool.

Cream the butter. Add the brown sugar and beat until light and fluffy. Add the egg yolks, one at a time, beating well after each addition. Beat in the cooled honey.

Sift together the flour, baking powder, salt, cinnamon, cloves and nutmeg. Beat the egg whites until stiff, but still moist. Stir the baking soda into the sour cream. Add the dry ingredients alternately with the sour cream to the creamed mixture. Stir in the walnuts. Fold in the stiffly beaten egg whites.

Spoon into the prepared pan. Bake at 160°C (325°F) for 40 minutes. Reduce the heat to 150°C (300°F) and bake for 30 to 35 minutes longer, or until a skewer inserted in the middle of the cake comes out clean. Cool in the pan for 20 minutes, then turn out onto a rack and cool completely.

Let the cake ripen for a day before using. Just before serving, sprinkle it with icing sugar and top it with sweetened whipped cream. Medivnyk stays deliciously moist for days.

Yields 12 servings.

Fruit Cake Icings

TRADITIONAL ALMOND PASTE

750	mL ground almonds	(3 cups)
3	egg yolks, slightly beaten	
15	mL corn syrup	(1 Tbs)
750	mL icing sugar	(3 cups)
10	mL almond extract	(2 tsp)

Combine all the ingredients in order and blend well, using your hands when necessary. Sprinkle a board lightly with icing sugar and turn the paste out onto it, kneading until smooth. Sprinkle on more icing sugar if the mixture becomes too sticky.

Roll to a 6 mm (1/4") thickness. Invert the cake over the paste and cut the paste to fit the top of the cake. If you wish to put paste on the sides as well, cut to fit. If the paste does not adhere well to the fruit cake, brush the cake surface with a thin covering of egg white.

Allow the cake to stand overnight before adding ornamental icing.
Yields about 750 mL (3 cups) paste, or enough to cover a 22.5 cm x 22.5 cm x 9 cm (9" x 9" x 3½") cake.

HOMEMADE ALMOND PASTE

This economical recipe contains neither ground almonds nor commercial paste, and it is delicious!

30	mL butter	(2 Tbs)
500	mL sifted icing sugar	(2 cups)
2	egg yolks	
15	mL almond extract	(1 Tbs)
	cream (optional)	

Cream the butter and icing sugar. Add the egg yolks and beat. Stir in the almond extract. If the mixture is not moist enough, add a few drops of cream.

After you have spread this paste over the cake, store the cake in a cold place. Let the almond paste dry before applying the decorative icing.
Yields about 375 mL (1½ cups) paste, or enough to cover a 2 L (9" x 5") cake.

ROYAL FROSTING

Spread this decorative frosting over the fruit cake after you have applied the almond paste. (For best results, let the almond paste set overnight on the cake before decorating with Royal Frosting.)

2	egg whites	
1	mL cream of tartar	(1/4 tsp)
550	mL sifted icing sugar	(2¼ cups)
2	mL vanilla	(½ tsp)

Beat the egg whites until frothy, add the cream of tartar and continue beating until very stiff. Sift the icing sugar through a fine sieve. Add a little at a time to the egg whites, beating thoroughly, first with an electric mixer, then with a wooden spoon. Beat in the vanilla. You should beat the frosting for about 5 minutes.
Yields 300 mL (1⅓ cups) frosting or enough to cover a 2 L (9" x 5") cake.

FLUFFY FRUIT CAKE ICING

After covering the top of the fruit cake with almond paste, let the cake sit overnight before applying this fluffy frosting.

250	mL shortening	(1 cup)
5	mL almond extract (or other flavouring)	(1 tsp)
5	mL vanilla	(1 tsp)
2	L icing sugar	(8 cups)
125	mL thin cream	(½ cup)

Cream the shortening well by beating with an electric mixer. Beat in the almond extract and vanilla. Continue beating and gradually add the icing sugar, beating until smooth. Gradually beat in the cream until the frosting is smooth and will spread easily (use a little more or less cream, depending on the consistency of the frosting).

Apply a thin layer of frosting to the paste-covered fruit cake. Let the frosting dry, then apply a second thick layer. Smooth the icing as you proceed with a knife dipped in hot water.
Yields about 875 mL (3½ cups) icing, or enough to frost a 3-layer wedding cake.

FRUIT CAKE GLAZE

This clear glaze is less perishable than icing and can be decorated with an arrangement of candied fruit. Cherries, pineapple and nuts such as whole almonds make an attractive and appealing decoration for both light and dark fruit cakes.

250	mL granulated sugar	(1 cup)
125	mL water	(½ cup)
75	mL corn syrup	(⅓ cup)

Mix together the sugar, water and corn syrup in a heavy saucepan. Stir over low heat until the sugar is dissolved. Increase the heat to medium-high and boil the mixture until it reaches the soft ball stage (115°C or 236°F).

Brush the glaze over top of the cake, reserving some of the liquid for the final glaze. Immediately arrange fruit and nuts on top and brush the final arrangement with the rest of the glaze.
Yields about 325 mL (1⅓ cups) glaze, or enough to decorate the tops of four medium fruit cakes.

PUDDINGS AND DESSERTS

INTRODUCTION

Whether it was a lumber camp pudding made from cornmeal and the year's small supply of raisins or an aristocratic maple sugar cake with nuts and sunflower seeds, desserts were of great importance to early Canadian Christmas dinners.

British settlers brought with them a variety of recipes for cakes, custards and puddings. Most important among them was plum pudding: it provided a much-needed link with Christmases in the Old Country.

In fact, early settlers' accounts suggest that a Christmas without plum pudding was not considered much of a Christmas at all. One of these settlers, a man named John Langton, whose letters describe life on the shore of Sturgeon Lake in Ontario in the 1830s, tried to make Plum Pudding on Christmas, even though ingredients were scarce. Although it was "a decided failure," he reported that the pudding was eaten anyway. And Paul Kane, a Canadian artist originally from Ireland, wrote about this unusual Christmas feast in Edmonton in 1847. The Indians in the encampment which he was visiting provided him with what appears to be a very elaborate Christmas dinner, consisting of "boiled buffalo hump, boiled buffalo calf, dried moose nose, white fish, buffalo tongue, beavers' tails, roast wild goose, piles of potatoes, turnips and bread." But despite the lavish meal, Kane still lamented that there were no "pies, puddings or blanc manges."

When the necessary ingredients were not to be had, settlers improvised. Apples and pumpkins were substituted for unavailable ingredients, and unusual (and delicious)

variations of the old favourites resulted.

The recipes in this chapter both reflect the ingenuity of those early settlers and pay homage to some of the traditional desserts they brought with them to their new land.

PLUM PUDDING

375	mL diced mixed candied peel	(1½ cups)
1 125	L seedless raisins	(4½ cups)
500	mL currants	(2 cups)
175	mL chopped candied cherries	(¾ cup)
300	mL orange juice or brandy	(1¼ cups)
375	mL all-purpose flour	(1½ cups)
7	mL baking powder	(1½ tsp)
2	mL salt	(½ tsp)
5	mL cinnamon	(1 tsp)
2	mL ground allspice	(½ tsp)
2	mL ground cloves	(½ tsp)
3	eggs	
500	mL lightly packed brown sugar	(2 cups)
500	mL finely chopped beef suet	(2 cups)
500	mL fine white bread crumbs	(2 cups)
10	mL grated lemon rind	(2 tsp)
45	mL lemon juice	(3 Tbs)
2	small chopped apples, unpeeled	
250	mL blanched slivered almonds	(1 cup)
50	mL brandy for flaming (optional)	(¼ cup)

Combine the peel, raisins, currants, cherries and orange juice or brandy. (Use a glass bowl if possible.) Cover and let sit overnight.

Prepare three 1 L (1 quart) moulds or one 3 L (3 quart) mould by greasing and sprinkling with granulated sugar.

Sift together the flour, baking powder, salt and spices. Drain the fruit well, reserving the liquid. Combine the fruit and flour mixtures thoroughly.

Beat the eggs well. Add the brown sugar and suet and beat together well. Stir in the bread crumbs. Add the lemon rind, lemon juice and the reserved liquid from fruit. Stir in the chopped apples, fruit and almonds, mixing only to blend.

Turn the batter into the prepared moulds and cover with a double thickness of wax paper and foil and tie securely with string.

Place on a rack in a large pot. Pour boiling water around the moulds to two-thirds of the way up the moulds. Cover tightly and steam for 3 to 4 hours, or until the top of the pudding is no longer sticky.

Remove the moulds from the water. Let the pudding set in the moulds for about 5 minutes, then turn out onto a warm platter. Make sure the platter is heatproof if you are going to flame the pudding. Serve hot accompanied by Hard Sauce, Rich Caramel Sauce or Cream Dressing (see recipes at the end of this chapter).

To flame the pudding, warm the brandy in a small saucepan. Do not let it boil. Avert your face, ignite the brandy with a match and immediately pour it over the warm pudding, basting the pudding while it flames.
Yields 18 servings.

Note: Plum Pudding is good if made 2 to 4 weeks ahead of time and refrigerated until needed. To reheat for serving, return the pudding to the mould and steam it covered for 1½ hours, or until heated through.

STEAMED FIG PUDDING

250	mL ground dried figs	(1 cup)
175	mL butter	(¾ cup)
250	mL granulated sugar	(1 cup)
2	eggs	
500	mL all-purpose flour	(2 cups)
5	mL baking powder	(1 tsp)
2	mL salt	(½ tsp)
5	mL mace	(1 tsp)
5	mL cinnamon	(1 tsp)
175	mL orange juice	(¾ cup)
5	mL vanilla	(1 tsp)
125	mL blanched slivered almonds	(½ cup)

Grease two 1 L (1 quart) pudding moulds and sprinkle with granulated sugar.

Clip the stems from the figs before grinding them in a food processor, meat grinder or blender.

Cream the butter, add the sugar and cream thoroughly together. Beat the eggs, add to the creamed mixture and beat well. Stir in the figs. Sift together the flour, baking powder, salt and spices, then add the dry ingredients, alternately with the orange juice, to the first mixture. Stir in the vanilla and almonds.

Turn the batter into the prepared moulds and cover with a double thickness of wax paper and foil. Tie securely.

Place on a rack in a large pot. Pour boiling water around the moulds to two-thirds of the way up the moulds. Steam for 2½ to 3 hours, or until the top of the pudding is no longer sticky.

Remove the moulds from the water. Let the puddings set in the moulds for about five minutes, then turn out onto a warm platter and serve hot. Serve with Foamy Orange Sauce or Rich Caramel Sauce (see recipes at the end of this chapter).
Yields 12 servings.

STEAMED CARROT PUDDING

Although the grated vegetables were probably first used as filler in this German interpretation of Plum Pudding, they do add a great deal to the texture and taste of the pudding.

500	mL chopped suet	(2 cups)
375	mL lightly packed brown sugar	(1½ cups)
15	mL corn syrup	(1 Tbs)
1	beaten egg	
250	mL grated raw carrot	(1 cup)
250	mL grated raw potato	(1 cup)
500	mL all-purpose flour	(2 cups)
5	mL salt	(1 tsp)
2	mL cinnamon	(½ tsp)
2	mL ground allspice	(½ tsp)
0.5	mL freshly grated nutmeg	(⅛ tsp)
250	mL seedless raisins	(1 cup)
250	mL currants	(1 cup)
375	mL mixed diced candied peel	(1½ cups)
375	mL whole candied cherries	(1½ cups)
150	mL chopped candied pineapple	(⅔ cup)
125	mL chopped walnuts	(½ cup)
250	mL fine dry bread crumbs	(1 cup)
5	mL baking soda	(1 tsp)
250	mL sour milk or buttermilk	(1 cup)
30	mL brandy	(2 Tbs)

Grease one 2 L (2 quart) or two 1 L (1 quart) moulds and sprinkle with granulated sugar. (Empty coffee tins are excellent for small puddings. This recipe fits nicely into three 500 g [1 lb] tins.)

Beat together the suet, brown sugar, corn syrup and egg. Stir in the grated carrot and potato.

In another bowl, sift together the flour, salt, cinnamon, all spice and nutmeg. Dredge the raisins, currants, peel, cherries, pineapple and walnuts with 125 mL (½ cup) of the sifted dry ingredients. Combine the remaining dry ingredients with the bread crumbs. Add the baking soda to the sour milk.

Add the dry ingredients to the suet mixture, alternately with the sour milk. Stir in the brandy and the prepared fruit and nuts.

Turn the batter into prepared moulds. The moulds should be no more than three-quarters full. Cover with a double thickness of wax paper and foil and tie securely with string.

Place on a rack in a large pot. Pour boiling water around the moulds to two-thirds of the way up the moulds. Cover tightly and steam for 3 hours, or until the top of the pudding is no longer sticky. Add more boiling water if necessary during this time, but make sure it just simmers in the pan.

Remove the moulds from the water. Let the pudding set in the moulds for about 5 minutes, then turn out onto a warm platter and serve hot with Fluffy White Pudding Sauce, Lemon Sauce or Hard Sauce (see recipes at the end of this chapter). Fluffy White Pudding Sauce is particularly good with this pudding.

Carrot Pudding freezes well. To reheat, thaw the pudding, return it to the mould, cover as before and steam for 1½ hours, or until heated through.
Yields 10 to 12 servings.

STEAMED CRANBERRY PUDDING

500	mL chopped cranberries	(2 cups)
175	mL chopped walnuts	(¾ cup)
125	mL chopped dried apricots	(½ cup)
500	mL all-purpose flour	(2 cups)
15	mL baking powder	(1 Tbs)
5	mL salt	(1 tsp)
250	mL fine dry bread crumbs	(1 cup)
250	mL lightly packed brown sugar	(1 cup)
250	mL chopped suet	(1 cup)
2	eggs	
150	mL milk	(⅔ cup)
5	mL almond extract	(1 tsp)

Grease two 1 L (1 quart) moulds and sprinkle with granulated sugar.

Combine the cranberries, walnuts and apricots and dredge with 50 mL (¼ cup) of the flour. Sift the remaining flour, baking powder and salt together. Combine with the bread crumbs.

Beat together the brown sugar, suet and eggs. Add the dry ingredients alternately with the milk to the suet mixture. Stir in the almond extract and the floured fruit and walnuts, combining well.

Turn the batter into the prepared moulds. The moulds should be no more than three-quarters full. Cover with a double thickness of wax paper and foil and tie securely with string.

Place on a rack in a large pot. Pour boiling water around the moulds to two-thirds of the way up the moulds. Cover tightly and steam for 2 to 2½ hours, or until the top of the pudding is no longer sticky. Add more boiling water if necessary during this time, but make sure the water just simmers in the pan as the pudding steams.

Remove the moulds from the water. Let the pudding set in the moulds for about 5 minutes, then turn out onto a warm platter and serve hot with Caramel Sauce, Almond Sauce or Hard Sauce (see recipes at the end of this chapter). If you are using Hard Sauce, try substituting 30 mL (2 Tbs) apricot brandy for the flavouring.

Yields 12 servings.

CRANBERRY SHERBET

Serve at the end of a heavy meal or between two rich courses as a light interlude to refresh the palate.

1	L cranberries	(4 cups)
500	mL water	(2 cups)
1	envelope unflavoured gelatin	
250	mL cold sauterne, fruity wine or cold water	(1 cup)
500	mL granulated sugar	(2 cups)
10	mL grated lemon rind	(2 tsp)
45	mL lemon juice	(3 Tbs)

Wash the cranberries and place them in the water in a large saucepan. Boil for about 5 minutes, or until the skins pop.

Meanwhile, sprinkle the gelatin over the sauterne and let stand for 5 minutes to soften.

Force the cooked cranberries through a sieve, discarding the skins. Return the cranberry purée to the saucepan. Add the sugar and softened gelatin mixture. Heat and stir until the gelatin and sugar dissolve. Cool. Stir in the lemon rind and juice. Pour into a metal pan, cover with foil and place in the freezer.

Freeze for 3 hours, until firm. Place in a chilled bowl and beat with an electric beater until mushy. Return to the metal pan and freeze again until firm, at least 3 hours, stirring two or three times during that time.

Yields 8 servings.

CREAMY CRANBERRY MOUSSE

This smooth creamy dessert can be made days before a dinner party. Served with a plate of Christmas cookies, it provides a light and unusual conclusion to a hearty holiday dinner.

250	mL fresh or frozen cranberries	(1 cup)
125	mL water	(½ cup)
250	mL granulated sugar	(1 cup)
30	mL grated orange rind	(2 Tbs)
125	mL cold orange juice	(½ cup)
1	envelope unflavoured gelatin	
4	eggs, separated	
125	mL granulated sugar	(½ cup)
250	mL heavy cream	(1 cup)
	additional sweetened whipped cream	
	red and green candied cherries	

Cook the cranberries in the water over high heat for 5 minutes, or until the skins pop. Then rub them through a sieve or put them through a food mill. Discard the skins. Add the 250 mL sugar and grated orange rind to the warm purée and stir until the sugar is dissolved. Cool.

In the top of a double boiler, combine the cold orange juice and gelatin and let sit for 5 minutes. Place over hot water and heat until warm, stirring often.

Meanwhile, beat the egg yolks together until blended. Gradually stir in 30 mL (2 Tbs) of the warm orange juice mixture. Then slowly pour the egg yolks back into the warm mixture, stirring constantly. Continue to stir over simmering water for about 4 minutes, or until thickened. Remove from the heat, cover with a piece of buttered wax paper and cool to room temperature.

Beat the egg whites until foamy. Gradually add the 125 mL sugar and continue beating until stiff, but still moist.

In a large bowl, whip the cream until it holds soft peaks. Fold the cranberry purée, orange mixture, then stiff egg whites into the whipped cream. Turn into a large serving bowl, cover and place in freezer.

The mousse will be cold enough to serve in 2 to 3 hours. If prepared ahead of time and frozen, remove from the freezer 30 minutes before serving.

Just before serving, garnish with piped whipped cream and pieces of red and green candied cherries. Yields 8 to 10 servings.

APPLE SNOW WITH CUSTARD SAUCE

Apple Snow will make good use of the late fall apples you may still have in the fruit cellar. It is a frothy dessert that can be made early in the day for an evening dinner party.

4	medium red apples	
125	mL water	(½ cup)
1	envelope unflavoured gelatin	
50	mL cold water	(¼ cup)
125	mL apple cider	(½ cup)
125	mL firmly packed brown sugar	(½ cup)
10	mL grated lemon rind	(2 tsp)
45	mL lemon juice	(3 Tbs)
	freshly grated nutmeg	
3	eggs, separated	
125	mL milk	(½ cup)
50	mL granulated sugar	(¼ cup)
0.5	mL salt	(⅛ tsp)
30	mL apple brandy	(2 Tbs)
75	mL whipping cream	(⅓ cup)

Core the apples and cut them into quarters. Cover and simmer slowly in the 125 mL water for 10 minutes, or until soft. Put through a food mill or sieve to remove skins and purée them. Set aside.

Meanwhile, soften the gelatin in the 50 mL cold water. Allow to stand for 5 minutes. Add the cider and stir over low heat until the gelatin is dissolved. Remove from the heat and add the brown sugar, lemon rind, lemon juice and nutmeg to taste. Chill until slightly thickened, about 30 to 45 minutes.

Beat the gelatin mixture until frothy. Beat the egg whites until stiff, but still moist. Fold the beaten egg whites and apple purée into the gelatin mixture. Chill for 2 hours, or until set.

To make the custard sauce, scald together the milk, granulated sugar and salt. Beat the egg yolks slightly and gradually stir warm milk into them. Return mixture to top of a double boiler and cook over low heat, stirring constantly for about 4 minutes, until the custard is thick enough to coat a spoon. Remove from the heat, cool and stir in the apple brandy. Chill.

Whip the cream and fold it into the custard sauce just before serving. Spoon some of the custard sauce over each serving of Apple Snow.
Yields 6 to 8 servings.

MINCEMEAT

Traditional English mincemeat is made by allowing the ingredients to steep for a month in Madeira, rum or brandy. The process is speeded up in this recipe by cooking the ingredients, then adding the spirit.
Mincemeat improves with age, so make it well in advance of the holiday season.

250	mL apple cider	(1 cup)
500	g peeled quartered apples	(1 lb)
750	mL currants	(3 cups)
750	mL seedless raisins	(3 cups)
550	mL diced mixed candied peel	(2¼ cups)
175	mL diced mixed candied fruit	(¾ cup)
1	L chopped beef suet	(4 cups)
550	mL firmly packed brown sugar	(2¼ cups)
250	mL chopped walnuts	(1 cup)
5	mL mace	(1 tsp)
5	mL cinnamon	(1 tsp)
5	mL ground cloves	(1 tsp)
5	mL freshly grated nutmeg	(1 tsp)
5	mL ground coriander or ground allspice	(1 tsp)
2	mL salt	(½ tsp)
10	mL grated lemon rind	(2 tsp)
45	mL lemon juice	(3 Tbs)
250	mL rum or brandy	(1 cup)

Boil the cider for about 5 minutes in a large heavy saucepan. Add the apples. Cook until soft, then mash.

Add the currants, raisins, candied peel, candied fruit, suet and sugar. Cook over low heat, stirring often, for 1 hour.

Add the remaining ingredients and stir well.Pour into hot sterilized sealers, leaving 12 mm (½ ") headspace. Process for 25 minutes in a boiling water bath. If left sealed, mincemeat will keep for a year.
Yields 2.5 L (5 pints) mincemeat.

Note: For a 1 L or 1.2 L (9" or 10") pie, use about 1 L (4 cups) mincemeat. Add 50 mL brandy to the filling if desired. Bake the pie at 230°C (450°F) for 10 minutes, then reduce the heat to 180°C (350°F) and bake for another 30 minutes or until golden brown.

GREEN TOMATO AND APPLE MINCEMEAT

Turn your late fall tomatoes into this beautiful mincemeat.

2	L cored chopped green tomatoes	(8 cups)
15	mL coarse pickling salt	(1 Tbs)
1	large orange	
2.5	L peeled cored chopped apples	(10 cups)
750	mL seedless raisins	(3 cups)
375	mL chopped suet	(1½ cups)
875	mL firmly packed brown sugar	(3½ cups)
125	mL cider vinegar	(½ cup)
10	mL cinnamon	(2 tsp)
5	mL freshly grated nutmeg	(1 tsp)
2	mL ground cloves	(½ tsp)
2	mL ground allspice	(½ tsp)
2	mL ground ginger	(½ tsp)

Optional

375	mL halved candied cherries	(1½ cups)
125	mL chopped candied citron peel	(½ cup)
125	mL brandy or rum	(½ cup)

Combine the tomatoes and salt and let sit for 1 hour.

Drain thoroughly. Cover with boiling water, let sit for 5 minutes, then drain off the water. Place the tomatoes in a large preserving kettle.

Grind the orange using a food processor fitted with a steel blade, a blender or a food grinder. Add the orange and the remaining ingredients, except the spirit, to the tomatoes in the preserving kettle. Bring to a boil, reduce the heat to medium and cook, uncovered, for about 35 to 40 minutes, until thickened. Stir frequently. Add the spirit.

Pour into hot sterilized sealers, leaving 12 mm (½") headspace. Process 25 minutes in a boiling water bath.
Yields 2 to 3 L (5 to 6 pints) mincemeat.

Note: For a 1 L or 1.2 L (9" or 10") pie, use 1 L (4 cups) of mincemeat, 250 mL (1 cup) sliced apples and 50 mL (¼ cup) brandy (if desired). Bake the pie at 230°C (450°F) for 10 minutes, then reduce the heat to 180°C (350°F) and bake for 30 minutes longer, or until golden brown.

FROZEN MINCEMEAT CREAM TARTS

250	mL heavy cream	(1 cup)
250	mL sour cream	(1 cup)
50	mL dark rum	(¼ cup)
250	mL Mincement (see page 29)	(1 cup)
24	baked 5 cm (2") tart shells (or smaller ones)	
	whipped cream	

Whip the cream until stiff. Fold in the sour cream and dark rum. Fold in the mincemeat. Spoon into tart shells and freeze 3 to 4 hours, or until firm.

Remove from the freezer 15 minutes before serving. Top each tart with a dab of whipped cream.
Yields 2 dozen tarts.

MINCEMEAT TRIFLE

Trifle is an elegant dessert that originated in Britain. Although sensational in appearance and taste, it is quite simple to make.

Custard

4	egg yolks	
50	mL granulated sugar	(¼ cup)
500	mL light cream	(2 cups)
7	mL vanilla	(1½ tsp)

Trifle

½	Old-Fashioned Pound Cake (see page 17)	
75	mL dry sherry	(⅓ cup)
500	mL Mincemeat (see page 29)	(2 cups)
300	mL heavy cream	(1¼ cups)
50	mL icing sugar	(¼ cup)
2	mL vanilla	(½ tsp)
	angelica, candied peel or candied cherries for garnish	

To prepare the custard, beat the egg yolks with the granulated sugar until thick. Heat the light cream in the top of a double boiler. Stirring constantly, pour the warm cream slowly into the beaten egg yolks, then return the whole mixture to the double boiler. Stirring constantly, cook over simmering water for about 4 minutes, until the custard thickly coats a spoon. Remove from the heat. Stir in the 7 mL vanilla. Press a piece of buttered wax paper onto the surface and chill for at least 3 hours.

To prepare the trifle, spread a thin layer of chilled custard in the bottom of a large glass serving bowl or glass cake pan.

Slice the pound cake into 1 cm (½") slices, and cut the slices into strips. Put a layer of cake strips on top of the custard in the bowl and sprinkle with half of the sherry. Spread half of the mincemeat over the cake. Pour 250 mL (1 cup) of the custard over the mincemeat. Repeat with the remaining cake, sherry, mincemeat and custard. Cover and chill overnight.

Just before serving, whip the cream until it holds soft peaks. Whip in the icing sugar and the 2 mL vanilla. Smooth half of the whipped cream on top of the trifle. Using a pastry bag, pipe the remaining whipped cream in rosettes around the edge. If you don't have a pastry bag, apply it in decorative swirls. Garnish with strips of angelica, candied peel or bits of candied cherry.
Yields 12 servings.

Variations:

Raspberry Trifle

Substitute two 283 g (10 oz) packages of frozen raspberries and 250 mL (1 cup) slivered almonds for the mincemeat. Thaw and thoroughly drain the raspberries and proceed as for Mincemeat Trifle. Reserve a few whole raspberries and some of the almonds for the garnish.

Strawberry Trifle

Substitute two 283 g (10 oz) packages of frozen strawberries and 250 mL (1 cup) coarsely chopped walnuts for the mincemeat. Thaw and thoroughly drain the strawberries and proceed as for Mincemeat Trifle. Reserve a few whole strawberries and some of the walnuts for the garnish.

PIE PASTRY

Sometimes called "Never-Fail Pastry," this recipe yields a tender and good pastry. Work gently and quickly for best results.

1 L pastry flour	(4 cups)
500 mL all-purpose flour	(2 cups)
7 mL salt	(1½ tsp)
450 g cold lard	(1 lb)
1 egg	
5 mL vinegar	(1 tsp)
cold water	

Mix the flour and salt together in a large bowl. Cut in the lard with a pastry blender or two knives until the mixture resembles coarse rolled oats.

Put the egg and vinegar in a 250 mL (1 cup) measure and fill with cold water. Stir well.

Add the liquid a bit at a time to the dry mixture, blending it in lightly with a fork. Gently finish combining the two mixtures with your hands. The dough may crumble slightly at this point. Wrap the dough tightly in wax paper and refrigerate for several hours, or overnight, to make the pastry easier to work with and more tender.

Remove from the refrigerator 30 minutes before rolling.

Yields enough for three 1 L (9") double-crust pies or six 1 L (9") pie shells.

WINTER PIE

Pioneer women probably put together the ingredients for this very old recipe when they did not have everything they needed to make mincemeat. Whatever its origins, it is well worth making.

250 mL seedless raisins	(1 cup)
125 mL finely grated carrot (packed into measure)	(½ cup)
125 mL granulated sugar	(½ cup)
15 mL cornstarch	(1 Tbs)
1 mL salt	(¼ tsp)
2 mL cinnamon	(½ tsp)
1 mL ground cloves	(¼ tsp)
1 mL freshly grated nutmeg	(¼ tsp)
50 mL apple juice or cider	(¼ cup)
125 mL hot water	(½ cup)
250 mL peeled coarsely chopped apple	(1 cup)
sufficient pastry for a 2-crust .75 L (8") pie	

Combine the raisins and carrot in a saucepan and add the sugar, cornstarch, salt and spices. Add the apple juice and water. Bring to a boil, reduce the heat and simmer for about 5 minutes. Add the apple and simmer for 15 minutes longer. Cool.

Preheat the oven to 230°C (450°F).

Line a pie plate with pastry. Spoon the filling into the bottom crust, heaping the filling up slightly in the middle. Moisten the pastry on the rim of the pie plate with cold water, cover with the top crust, trim and flute the edges firmly. Slash a few holes near the centre of the pie crust to allow steam to escape.

Bake at 230°C (450°F) for 10 minutes, then reduce the heat to 180°C (350°F) and bake for another 20 minutes, or until the pastry is golden brown.

Yields 5 to 6 servings.

PUMPKIN PIE

Pumpkin pie was often served at pioneer Christmas dinners, because many families still had healthy pumpkins in their root cellars in December. This recipe makes a particularly light and very delicious pumpkin pie.

250	mL evaporated milk	(1 cup)
2	eggs, separated	
175	mL firmly packed brown sugar	(¾ cup)
1	mL salt	(¼ tsp)
5	mL cinnamon	(1 tsp)
2	mL ground ginger	(½ tsp)
2	mL ground allspice	(½ tsp)
1	mL ground cloves	(¼ tsp)
	freshly grated nutmeg	
250	mL cooked pumpkin purée	(1 cup)
	sufficient pastry for a 1-crust 1 L (9") pie (see page 32)	
	sweetened whipped cream and sliced candied ginger for garnish	

Preheat the oven to 220°C (425°F).

Scald the milk in the top of a double boiler. Beat the egg yolks slightly. Pour the hot milk into the yolks, stirring constantly. Add the brown sugar and salt and return the mixture to the top of the double boiler. Cook, stirring constantly, for about 4 minutes, until the mixture coats a spoon. Remove from the heat.

Stir the spices into the pumpkin purée and fold the purée into the milk mixture.

Beat the egg whites until stiff, but still moist, and fold them into the pumpkin mixture.

Line a pie plate with pastry. Pour the pumpkin mixture into pie shell and bake at 220°C (425°F) for 15 minutes. Reduce the heat to 180°C (350°F) and bake for about 35 to 40 minutes longer, or until set. Cool. Pipe on sweetened whipped cream just before serving and garnish with slivers of candied ginger.
Yields 6 servings.

PUMPKIN-MINCEMEAT PIE

This combination pie appeared in wartime Canada, when nothing was wasted. Leftover fillings from two pies were simply combined into one. The result is a delicious and unusual pie in which the pumpkin counteracts the richness and sweetness of the mincemeat.

	sufficient pastry for a 1 crust 1 L (9") pie (see page 32)	
375	mL Mincemeat (see page 29)	(1½ cups)
	½ recipe Pumpkin Pie filling	
	sweetened whipped cream	

Preheat the oven to 220°C (425°F).

Line a pie plate with pastry. Spread the mincemeat in the bottom of the pie crust. Pour the pumpkin filling over the mincemeat and bake at 220°C(425°F) for 15 minutes. Reduce the heat to 180°C (350°F) and bake 35 to 40 minutes longer, or until set. Cool. Pipe on the sweetened whipped cream just before serving.
Yields 6 servings.

CRANBERRY PIE

Also called "Mock Cherry Pie," this is an old favourite at Christmas in many Canadian homes.

750	mL coarsely chopped raw cranberries	(3 cups)
250	mL lightly packed brown sugar	(1 cup)
30	mL water	(2 Tbs)
5	mL almond extract	(1 tsp)
	sufficient pastry for a 2-crust 1 L (9") pie (see page 32)	
15	mL quick-cooking tapioca	(1 Tbs)
30	mL butter	(2 Tbs)

Preheat the oven to 230°C (450°F).

Mix together the cranberries, brown sugar, water and almond extract.

Line a pie plate with half the pastry. Sprinkle half the tapioca over the bottom. Pour in the cranberry mixture. Sprinkle with the remaining tapioca and dot with butter.

Cover with a lattice top made from the rest of the pastry.

Bake for 10 minutes at 230°C (450°F) then reduce the heat to 180°C (350°F) and continue baking for 30 minutes, or until the crust is golden brown. Serve warm or at room temperature with sweetened whipped cream or vanilla ice cream.

Yields 6 to 8 servings.

MAPLE SUGAR PIE

Among French Canadians, two popular desserts for the holidays are Maple Sugar Pie and Maple Syrup Pie. This one from New Brunswick is not as rich or sweet as its name suggests.

500	mL maple sugar	(2 cups)
250	mL water	(1 cup)
250	mL heavy cream	(1 cup)
90	mL butter	(6 Tbs)
90	mL all-purpose flour	(6 Tbs)
125	mL chopped walnuts	(½ cup)
	sufficient pastry for a 1-crust 1 L (9") pie (see page 32)	
	whipped cream (optional)	

Combine the maple sugar and water in a saucepan. Bring to a boil, then reduce the heat and simmer for 10 minutes. Add the cream and simmer over low heat for 5 minutes, stirring constantly.

Melt the butter over low heat. Add the flour and stir over the heat for 5 minutes. Do not brown. Add to the maple sugar mixture and cook, stirring, for another 15 minutes over medium-low heat. Remove from the heat and add the chopped nuts. Cool.

Preheat the oven to 230°C (450F).

Line a pie plate with the pastry. Pour the filling into the crust and bake for 10 minutes at 230°C (450°F). Reduce the heat to 180°C (350°F) and bake for another 30 minutes. Serve at room temperature with whipped cream, if desired.

Yields 6 to 8 servings.

MAPLE SYRUP PIE

250	mL maple syrup	(1 cup)
125	mL water	(½ cup)
50	mL cornstarch	(¼ cup)
45	mL cold water	(3 Tbs)
50	mL butter	(¼ cup)
2	mL vanilla	(½ tsp)
50	mL chopped walnuts	(¼ cup)

sufficient pastry for a .75 L (8") shallow flan pan (see page 32)

Meringue

2	egg whites	
2	mL cream of tartar	(½ tsp)
50	mL granulated sugar	(¼ cup)
0.5	mL salt	(⅛ tsp)
2	mL vanilla	(½ tsp)
30	mL water	(2 Tbs)

Boil the maple syrup and water together in a saucepan for 5 minutes.

Meanwhile, dissolve the cornstarch in the cold water and add slowly to the boiling liquid, stirring constantly. Cook, stirring, for about 10 minutes, until the mixture becomes smooth and thick. Remove from the heat. Add the butter, vanilla and walnuts. Cool.

Preheat the oven to 230°C(450°F).

Line the flan pan with pastry. Pour the filling into the crust and bake for 10 minutes at 230°C. Reduce the heat to 180°C (350°F) and bake for 30 minutes longer, or until firm.

Remove the pie and increase the oven temperature to 190°C (375°F).

To make the meringue, beat the egg whites and cream of tartar together to form moist peaks. Very gradually beat in the sugar. Add the remaining ingredients and beat until stiff and shiny.

Spread the meringue over the filling, making sure the meringue touches the pastry rim all the way around. Swirl the meringue into points and bake for 12 to 15 minutes at 190°C, or until tips of the meringue become golden. Remove from the oven and cool slowly.

Yields 6 to 8 servings.

Variation:

Fill 12 tiny uncooked tart shells with filling and bake for about 20 minutes at 190°C (375°F). Cover with meringue and brown as for Maple Syrup Pie.

LEMON BUTTER

Popular as a filling for tiny tarts at Christmas, lemon butter is sometimes called lemon cheese or lemon curd. It keeps well in a jar stored in the refrigerator and is also delicious as a cake filling or spread for toast.

3	eggs	
10	mL grated lemon rind	(2 tsp)
75	mL lemon juice	(⅓ cup)
250	mL granulated sugar	(1 cup)
75	mL butter	(⅓ cup)

Beat the eggs slightly in the top of a double boiler. Stir in the lemon rind, lemon juice, sugar and butter. Cook, stirring constantly, over simmering water until the mixture resembles soft custard. (It will thicken somewhat on cooling.)

Chill before using.

If used as a filling for tarts, spoon lemon butter into baked tart shells just before serving and top with whipped cream.

Yields sufficient filling for about eighteen 5 cm (2") tart shells.

WINTER FRUIT SALAD

This fruit salad should be made a few hours or a day ahead of time so that the flavours can mingle. Serve it chilled, with or without Cream Dressing, as a refreshing start to a brunch or as a light dessert after a heavy meal.

1	lemon	
5	oranges	
175	mL granulated sugar	(¾ cup)
250	mL water	(1 cup)
50	mL orange liqueur	(¼ cup)
1	pink grapefruit	
3	firm winter pears	
3	Red Delicious apples	
2	bananas	
500	mL halved, seeded red grapes	(2 cups)
283	g frozen strawberries or raspberries	(10 oz)

Squeeze the juice from the lemon and 2 of the oranges into a saucepan. Add the sugar and water. Stir over medium heat until the sugar is dissolved. Bring to a boil and boil uncovered for 5 minutes. Remove from the heat and cool. Add the liqueur.

Peel and remove the white membrane from the 3 remaining oranges and the grapefruit. Cut them into 5 cm (2") pieces. Cut and core the pears and apples, leaving the skin on, and chop them into 5 cm pieces. Slice the bananas. Place the prepared fruit and grapes in a glass serving bowl. Pour in the fruit and sugar syrup and mix gently. Chill.

Thaw the strawberries or raspberries only until they separate nicely. Add them to the rest of the chilled fruit 30 minutes before serving. Serve with Cream Dressing (see page 38), if desired.
Yields 15 servings.

Sauces

HARD SAUCE

Delicious with Steamed Cranberry Pudding or Plum Pudding.

50	mL butter	(¼ cup)
250	mL icing sugar	(1 cup)
5	mL lemon extract	(1 tsp)
1	egg white	

Cream butter until very light. Gradually add the icing sugar and continue to cream until fluffy. Gradually add the lemon extract. Beat the egg white until stiff and fold it into the butter and sugar mixture. Place in a small serving dish and chill until hard.
Yields about 300 mL (1¼ cups) sauce.

Variations:

Brandy Hard Sauce

Omit the egg white. Substitute 30 mL (2 Tbs) brandy for the lemon extract and proceed as for Hard Sauce. You may also add 5 mL (1 tsp) vanilla to this recipe, if desired.

Almond Sauce

This sauce is excellent with Steamed Cranberry Pudding.
Proceed as for Hard Sauce recipe, substituting 2 mL (½ tsp) almond extract for the lemon extract and leaving in the egg white.

RICH CARAMEL SAUCE

Good with most steamed puddings.

250	mL firmly packed brown sugar	(1 cup)
7	mL cornstarch	(1½ tsp)
250	mL light cream	(1 cup)
50	mL butter	(¼ cup)
5	mL vanilla	(1 tsp)
30	mL brandy	(2 Tbs)

Combine the brown sugar and cornstarch in the top of a double boiler. Gradually add the cream and stir until the sugar is dissolved. Place over simmering water. Add the butter and cook, stirring constantly, until the mixture is smooth and thickens slightly. Cook for a few minutes longer, stirring often, about 10 minutes in all.

Remove from the heat and stir in the vanilla and brandy. Serve hot over hot steamed pudding.
Yields about 500 mL (2 cups) sauce.

FOAMY ORANGE SAUCE

This goes well with Steamed Fig Pudding

125	mL soft butter	(½ cup)
250	mL icing sugar	(1 cup)
1	egg, beaten	
30	mL orange juice	(2 Tbs)
5	mL finely grated orange rind	(1 tsp)

Cream the butter, add the sugar and beat until light and fluffy. Beat in the egg. Very gradually add the orange juice, a drop at a time. Stir in the orange rind. Beat the sauce until light and fluffy. Serve immediately.
Yields about 375 mL (1½ cups) sauce.

FLUFFY WHITE PUDDING SAUCE

This beautifully creamy sauce complements any steamed pudding. It is also delicious with hot mincemeat tarts.

125	mL butter	(½ cup)
2	eggs, separated	
50	mL all-purpose flour	(¼ cup)
250	mL granulated sugar	(1 cup)
250	mL milk	(1 cup)
250	mL heavy cream	(1 cup)
5	mL vanilla	(1 tsp)
	freshly grated nutmeg	

Mix the butter and egg yolks together in the top of a double boiler. Add the flour and sugar and blend well. Gradually stir in the milk. Cook over medium heat, stirring constantly, until the mixture is like a thin custard, about 10 minutes in all. Cool.

Whip the cream. Beat the egg whites until stiff. When the sauce is cool, add the vanilla and carefully fold in the whipped cream and beaten egg whites. Refrigerate until needed. The sauce can be made a day in advance, if necessary.

Top with a light sprinkling of freshly grated nutmeg before serving.
Yields about 750 mL (3 cups) sauce.

LEMON SAUCE

Rich with the flavour of lemon, this rather clear thin sauce is delicious with Steamed Carrot Pudding or Steamed Cranberry Pudding.

250	mL granulated sugar	(1 cup)
30	mL cornstarch	(2 Tbs)
1	mL salt	(¼ tsp)
500	mL boiling water	(2 cups)
45	mL butter	(3 Tbs)
45	mL lemon juice	(3 Tbs)
2	mL grated lemon rind	(½ tsp)

Mix the sugar, cornstarch and salt together in the top of a double boiler. Slowly add the boiling water to the mixture, stirring constantly. Cook over hot water for 15 minutes, or until the sauce becomes clear and thickens slightly. When ready to serve, remove from the heat and add butter, lemon juice and lemon rind. Stir until the butter melts. Serve hot.
Yields about 750 mL (3 cups) sauce.

CREAM DRESSING

Good with most steamed puddings and Winter Fruit Salad.

15	mL all-purpose flour	(1 Tbs)
75	mL granulated sugar	(⅓ cup)
1	egg	
75	mL dry white wine	(⅓ cup)
30	mL orange liqueur	(2 Tbs)
15	mL lemon juice	(1 Tbs)
50	mL orange juice	(¼ cup)
125	mL heavy cream	(½ cup)

In the top of a double boiler, mix the flour and sugar. Beat the egg until foamy and add to the flour mixture. While stirring, gradually add the wine, liqueur and strained fruit juices to the flour mixture. Cook over simmering water, stirring until thickened, about 10 minutes in all. Cool.

Whip the cream and fold it into the cooled mixture.
Yields about 500 mL (2 cups) dressing.

COOKIES

INTRODUCTION

In the minds of Canada's German settlers, Christmas cookies were for children. Elaborately decorated cookies were hung on boughs of evergreen, and later on Christmas trees, for children to enjoy and – of course – to eat.

The predominantly German custom of making cookies at Christmas caught on very quickly, so that despite the shortage of ingredients, most pioneer housewives made sugar cookies or gingerbread for the holidays.

Today, most people make at least one or two types of cookies, while some make dozens.

This chapter features a wide variety of traditional Christmas recipes, some of which were brought to Canada from other lands, including the well-established Scottish shortbread. The recipes are arranged according to when they might be prepared in the weeks before Christmas, with those which require ripening time appearing first. Unless otherwise specified, store the cookies in air-tight containers, preferably in a cool dry place.

BASELER LECKERLI

This chewy German cookie should be made five weeks before Christmas to allow ripening.

1.3	L all-purpose flour	(5¼ cups)
625	mL granulated sugar	(2½ cups)
10	mL baking powder	(2 tsp)
5	mL cinnamon	(1 tsp)
1	mL ground cloves	(¼ tsp)
30	mL honey	(2 Tbs)
15	mL water or brandy	(1 Tbs)
375	mL blanched chopped almonds	(1½ cups)
375	mL diced mixed candied peel	(1½ cups)
4	eggs	

Icing

150	mL icing sugar	(⅔ cup)
1	mL almond extract	(¼ tsp)
10	mL water	(2 tsp)

Grease a cookie sheet that has 1 cm (½") sides. Preheat the oven to 180°C (350°F).

Sift the flour, sugar, baking powder, cinnamon and cloves into a large bowl. Mix in the honey and water (or brandy). Mix in the almonds and candied peel. Make a well in the middle of the mixture and in it place the eggs.

Using your hands, work the eggs into the flour mixture one at a time. Knead well in the bowl, then turn out onto a board and continue to knead until the dough holds together and can be formed into a ball. (This step takes a while.)

Spread onto the greased sheet and, using a rolling pin, evenly cover the entire sheet with the dough.

Bake for 10 to 15 minutes, or until light golden.

While the cookie is baking, prepare the icing by combining the icing sugar, almond extract and water and stirring until smooth. Spread onto the warm cookie. Cool. Cut into small squares and store in an air-tight container.

Yields 5 dozen squares.

CHRISTMAS FRUIT COOKIES

These German fruit cookies are a favourite in Mennonite homes. Make them well before Christmas to let their spicy flavour ripen.

125 mL shortening	(½ cup)
125 mL butter	(½ cup)
375 mL firmly packed brown sugar	(1½ cups)
2 eggs, beaten	
5 mL lemon extract	(1 tsp)
50 mL orange juice	(¼ cup)
625 mL all-purpose flour	(2½ cups)
5 mL baking soda	(1 tsp)
2 mL salt	(½ tsp)
5 mL cinnamon	(1 tsp)
2 mL ground cloves	(½ tsp)
2 mL freshly grated nutmeg	(½ tsp)
500 mL chopped seedless raisins	(2 cups)
325 mL chopped dates	(1⅓ cups)
150 mL chopped candied cherries	(⅔ cup)
125 mL chopped candied pineapple	(½ cup)
175 mL citron peel	(¾ cup)
250 mL finely chopped pecans	(1 cup)
250 mL finely chopped walnuts	(1 cup)
250 mL finely chopped filberts	(1 cup)

Grease baking sheets. Preheat the oven to 180°C (350°F).

Cream the shortening and butter, add the sugar and beat until light and fluffy. Beat in the eggs, lemon extract and orange juice.

Sift together the flour, baking soda, salt and spices.

Chop all the fruit and nuts by hand or in a blender or food processor. (Do not process candied fruit too long, or it will become mushy.) Mix 125 mL (½ cup) of the dry ingredients with fruit mixture.

Stir the rest of the dry ingredients into the first creamed mixture. Add the floured fruit and nuts and mix well.

Drop by spoonfuls 5 cm (2") apart on greased baking sheets. Bake for 12 to 15 minutes, or until light brown. Cool on racks, then store in air-tight container for 3 to 4 weeks.

Yields 12 dozen cookies.

FORGOTTEN MERINGUES

One of the simplest cookies to make, these meringues look quite elegant on a plate of holiday dainties. Since they do not freeze well and are best fresh, make them no more than a week before serving.

3 egg whites	
1 mL cream of tartar	(¼ tsp)
250 mL powdered fruit sugar	(1 cup)
food colouring (optional)	

Line three cookie sheets with foil. Preheat the oven to 190°C (375°F).

Beat the egg whites until slightly foamy, add the cream of tartar and continue beating. When frothy, gradually add the sugar, a little at a time, beating until just stiff and glossy. (If you beat the mixture too long after it is stiff, the meringues may crumble.)

For a colourful selection of cookies, divide the mixture into three bowls and carefully add a few drops of red food colouring to one part and a few drops of green food colouring to another. Drop in small spoonfuls onto the prepared sheets.

Place in the oven and turn the heat off immediately. Do not open the oven door until the next morning. Store in an air-tight container.

Yields about 5 dozen cookies.

THIMBLE COOKIES

"Thumbprint Cookies" or "Swedish Tea Rings" are other names for this old-fashioned cookie found in many local cookbooks from across the country.

125	mL butter	(½ cup)
125	mL granulated sugar	(½ cup)
1	egg, separated	
5	mL vanilla	(1 tsp)
250	mL all-purpose flour	(1 cup)
150	mL finely chopped walnuts	(¾ cup)
	jelly or jam	

Lightly grease baking sheets. Preheat the oven to 180°C (350°F).

Cream the butter, add the sugar and beat until light and fluffy. Add the egg yolk and beat well. Add the vanilla. Gradually stir in the flour until the dough is smooth.

Shape the dough into tiny balls. Dip each ball into the unbeaten egg white, then in chopped nuts. Using a floured thimble, make a dent in the centre of each cookie.

Place on the prepared sheets. Bake for 5 minutes, then dent again with the thimble and repair sides of cookies if necessary. Bake for 12 minutes longer, or until set. Cool on a rack and fill each depression with a bit of jelly or jam.
Yields 3 dozen cookies.

OLD-FASHIONED CHEWY GINGER COOKIES

These cookies and the Rolled Ginger Cookies which follow were brought to Canada by German settlers. Old-Fashioned Ginger Cookies are delicious at Christmas and all year round.

125	mL lard	(½ cup)
250	mL granulated sugar	(1 cup)
2	eggs	
250	mL molasses	(1 cup)
875	mL all-purpose flour	(3½ cups)
6	mL baking soda	(1¼ tsp)
15	mL ground ginger	(1 Tbs)
5	mL ground cloves	(1 tsp)
2	mL cinnamon	(½ tsp)
	granulated sugar	

Cream the lard and sugar together until light and fluffy. Beat in the eggs, one at a time, and then the molasses.

Sift together the flour, soda and spices. Mix the dry ingredients in three parts into the creamed mixture. Knead the dough gently until smooth and refrigerate for 2 hours.

Lightly grease baking sheets. Preheat the oven to 190°C (375°F).

Form the dough into 3 cm (1¼") balls and roll them in granulated sugar. Place on the prepared sheets and bake for 10 to 12 minutes, or until set.
Yields 5 dozen cookies.

ROLLED GINGER COOKIES

The dough for these Ginger Cookies can be rolled to make gingerbread men or houses. For gingerbread men, imbed raisins or currants in the dough before baking, or pipe on the decorative icing after the cookies have cooled.

175	mL molasses	(¾ cup)
375	mL lightly packed brown sugar	(1½ cups)
250	mL butter	(1 cup)
15	mL ground ginger	(1 Tbs)
1	mL gound cloves	(¼ tsp)
5	mL baking soda	(1 tsp)
50	mL hot water	(¼ cup)
1	egg, well beaten	
2	mL salt	(½ tsp)
1.375	L all-purpose flour	(5½ cups)

Decorative Icing (optional)

500	mL icing sugar	(2 cups)
1½	egg whites	
7	mL white vinegar	(1½ tsp)

To make the cookies, combine the molasses, brown sugar, butter, ginger and cloves in a large saucepan. Stir over low heat until the sugar is dissolved and the butter melts. Bring to a boil. Let cool.

Dissolve the baking soda in hot water. Add it to the molasses mixture. Then stir in the egg, salt and flour. If the dough is too sticky, add a little more flour. Wrap in wax paper and chill for several hours or overnight.

Lightly grease baking sheets. Preheat the oven to 180°C (350°F).

The dough will be very hard when it comes out of the refrigerator. Either let it return to room temperature or cut slices from the chilled dough and roll them between two pieces of wax paper. Roll the pieces of dough out to a thickness of 3 mm (⅛″) and cut out into desired shapes.

Bake on the prepared sheets for 8 to 10 minutes, or until lightly browned. Cool on racks and store in an air-tight container.

To make the decorative icing, combine the sugar and egg whites and beat with an electric mixer at low speed until the mixture starts to hold its shape. Add vinegar and beat at high speed until stiff and glossy. Since this hardens quickly, apply decorative sugar or candies immediately, and do your piping fairly quickly.

Yields 15 dozen cookies.

OLD-FASHIONED SUGAR COOKIES

Through the years, most cookie jars have been graced by good old-fashioned sugar cookies. Although they are delicious all year round, these sugar cookies will be an attractive and tasty addition to your Christmas trays when garnished with bits of candied cherries, peel, nuts or coloured sugar or decorated with an icing glaze.

250	mL butter	(1 cup)
125	mL lightly packed brown sugar	(½ cup)
125	mL granulated sugar	(½ cup)
1	egg	
2	mL vanilla	(½ tsp)
500	mL all-purpose flour	(2 cups)
5	mL baking soda	(1 tsp)
5	ml cream of tartar	(1 tsp)
	coloured sugar, candied fruit or decorating candies for garnish	

Icing Glaze (optional)

250 mL icing sugar	(1 cup)
15-20 mL milk	(1½ Tbs)
food colouring	

Cream the butter. Add the brown sugar and granulated sugar and beat until light and fluffy. Beat in the egg and then the vanilla.

Sift together the flour, baking soda and cream of tartar. Gradually add the dry ingredients to the creamed mixture, stirring only until thoroughly mixed. Divide the dough into two, wrap each half in wax paper and chill for 3 hours or longer.

Preheat the oven to 190°C (375°F).

Roll dough out to a thickness of 6 mm (¼") or less, working with a bit at a time. Cut the cookies into the desired shapes and, using a metal spatula, place on baking sheets. Leave a space of about 4 cm (1½") between the cookies for them to expand. Decorate as desired. (If you wish to decorate with icing glaze, do so after the cookies have been baked and cooled.)

Bake for 8 minutes, or until lightly browned. Cool flat on racks. Prepare the glaze, if desired, and ice the cookies. Store in an air-tight container.

To make the icing glaze, combine the icing sugar and milk in a small bowl. Stir until smooth. For a green or pink glaze, add a few drops of food colouring and mix well. Spread the glaze on the top of the cookies after they have been baked and cooled.

If you wish to garnish the glaze with coloured candies or bits of cherries, do so immediately before the icing becomes too hard.

Yields 3 dozen 9 cm (3½") cookies.

CHOCOLATE RUM BALLS

There are many recipes for these perennial Christmas favourites. This recipe, containing almonds, is a bit different and well worth the trouble of grating chocolate.

250 mL blanched ground almonds	(1 cup)
250 mL sifted icing sugar	(1 cup)
6 mL powdered instant coffee	(1¼ tsp)
3 squares unsweetened chocolate	(3 oz)
75 mL dark rum	(5 Tbs)
15 mL milk	(1 Tbs)
125 mL dark chocolate vermicelli	(½ cup)

Place the almonds in a large bowl and sift in the icing sugar and instant coffee. Grate the chocolate squares, using a grater or food processor fitted with a steel blade or a blender. Stir the finely grated chocolate into almond and sugar mixture. Sprinkle 45 mL (3 Tbs) of the rum and all of the milk over the dry ingredients. Mix until the mixture is evenly moistened and is a uniform dark brown. Chill for 10 minutes.

Remove from the refrigerator, shape into a ball and knead several times. Using your hands, roll the dough into 2 cm (¾") balls. Dip each ball into the remaining rum, shake off the excess moisture and roll the balls in vermicelli to coat thickly. Place on wax paper and dry for 1 hour.

Place in air-tight container and refrigerate. Let the Chocolate Rum Balls ripen for a few days before serving.

Yields 2½ dozen rum balls.

PECAN CRESCENTS

Vanilla Sugar

¼ vanilla bean	
250 mL icing sugar	(1 cup)

Cookies

250 mL butter	(1 cup)
125 mL icing sugar	(½ cup)
10 mL vanilla	(2 tsp)
500 mL all-purpose flour	(2 cups)
2 mL salt	(½ tsp)
500 mL finely chopped pecans	(2 cups)

To prepare the vanilla sugar, cut the piece of vanilla bean into several pieces. Combine it with about 45 mL (3 Tbs) of the icing sugar in a blender and blend at top speed until well blended, or pound together with a mortar and pestle. Add to the rest of the icing sugar. Let the vanilla sugar sit for a day or two, so that the flavours blend together.

When you are ready to make the cookies, preheat the oven to 160°C (325°F).

Cream the butter, add the icing sugar gradually and beat until light and fluffy. Add the vanilla. Sift the flour and salt together and add to the creamed mixture. Fold in the pecans.

Using 15 mL (1 Tbs) dough for each cookie, shape into crescents.

Bake on ungreased sheets for 25 minutes, or until light golden-brown.

Gently cover the warm cookies with the vanilla sugar. Cool completely on racks. Yields 6 dozen cookies.

Variation:

Almond or Filbert Crescents

Substitute 500 mL (2 cups) ground blanched almonds or filberts for the pecans and proceed as for Pecan Crescents.

DATE DAINTIES

These uncooked tidbits are fun and easy for children to make and eat.

250 mL peanut butter	(1 cup)
25 mL butter	(1½ Tbs)
250 mL icing sugar	(1 cup)
250 mL finely chopped dates	(1 cup)
175 mL finely chopped walnuts	(¾ cup)
6 squares semi-sweet chocolate	(6 oz)
2 cm square piece of paraffin wax	(¾")

Cream the peanut butter and butter together. Add the icing sugar and cream thoroughly. Add the dates and nuts and mix well. Using a small spoonful of the mixture, shape into fingers. (Dampening your hands will make shaping the dough easier.) Chill.

Melt the chocolate and wax in the top of a double boiler. Using a metal knitting needle, dip each finger in the melted chocolate. Place on wax paper to set and cool. Store in an air-tight container in the refrigerator. Yields 5 dozen dainties.

ICE-BOX COOKIES

125 mL butter	(½ cup)
250 mL granulated sugar	(1 cup)
1 egg	
30 mL lemon juice	(2 Tbs)
500 mL all-purpose flour	(2 cups)
2 mL baking soda	(½ tsp)
2 mL salt	(½ tsp)
coloured sugar or decorator candies	

Cream the butter, add the sugar and beat until fluffy. Add the egg and beat until very light. Stir in the lemon juice.

Sift together the flour, baking soda and salt and mix well with the creamed mixture. Shape the dough into a roll about 5 cm (2") in diameter, wrap in wax paper and chill for about 1 hour.

Remove from the refrigerator and roll slightly on the counter so that cookies will be round when cut. Chill several hours more, or overnight.

Grease baking sheets. Preheat the oven to 190°C (375°F).

With a sharp knife (an electric knife works well), cut the roll into slices about 3 mm (⅛") thick. Leaving room for the cookies to expand, put them on the prepared sheets and sprinkle with coloured sugar or tiny decorator candies.

Bake for about 10 minutes, or until firm. Remove from the oven and cool the cookies on racks. Rolls of dough may be stored in the refrigerator for as long as ten days, or they may be frozen for as long as a month. Yields about 6 dozen cookies.

Variations:

Cherry Nut Cookies

Add 250 mL (1 cup) finely slivered almonds and 150 mL (⅔ cup) diced candied cherries to the dough and proceed as for Ice-Box cookies, omitting the garnish.

Lemon Cocoanut Cookies

Add 15 mL (1 Tbs) grated lemon rind and 150 mL (⅔ cup) grated cocoanut to the dough and proceed as for Ice-Box Cookies.

Peppermint Pinwheels

Divide the dough into two. To one half add 2 mL (½ tsp) peppermint extract and a few drops red food colouring. Roll each half of the dough between two sheets of wax paper to a 40 cm x 25 cm (16" x 10") rectangle. Remove the top sheets of the wax paper. Invert the pink layer onto the plain layer and peel off the remaining wax paper. With the two rectangles of dough on top of each other, roll up tightly, jelly-roll fashion, starting at the long side. Slice and bake. These are pretty without any further decoration.

Chocolate Peppermint Pinwheels

Divide the dough into two. To one half add 2 mL (½ tsp) peppermint extract and 2 squares (2 oz) unsweetened chocolate, melted and cooled. Proceed as for Peppermint Pinwheels.

FLORENTINES

Florentines make an elegant addition to a holiday cookie tray. This version features a particularly interesting combination of chocolate and orange peel.

50 mL finely chopped sultana raisins	(¼ cup)
150 mL diced candied orange peel	(⅔ cup)
75 mL blanched slivered almonds	(⅓ cup)
50 mL all-purpose flour	(¼ cup)
45 mL butter	(3 Tbs)
50 mL granulated sugar	(¼ cup)
125 mL heavy cream	(½ cup)
5 mL lemon juice	(1 tsp)
250 mL semi-sweet chocolate chips	(1 cup)
tiny decorating candies	

Grease and flour two baking sheets. Preheat the oven to 180°C (350°F).

Combine the raisins , peel and nuts and dredge with the flour.

Combine the butter, sugar and cream in a saucepan and bring to a boil. Remove from the heat and stir in floured fruit and nuts and the lemon juice.

Drop by spoonfuls onto the prepared sheets, leaving room for the cookies to expand. Bake for about 10 minutes, or until golden brown. Cool on the sheets for 2 minutes, then transfer the cookies to racks to cool completely.

Melt the chocolate over hot water. Turn the cookies upside down and brush melted chocolate onto the bottoms. Sprinkle tiny decorating candies on top of the chocolate.
Yields about 2 dozen cookies.

LEMON COOKIES

250 mL butter	(1 cup)
115 g cream cheese	(4 oz)
250 mL granulated sugar	(1 cup)
1 egg	
25 mL grated lemon rind	(1½ Tbs)
50 mL lemon juice	(4 Tbs)
875 mL all-purpose flour	(3½ cups)
5 mL baking powder	(1 tsp)
coloured sugar (optional)	

Cream together the butter and cream cheese. Gradually add the sugar and beat until light and fluffy. Beat in the egg. Stir in the lemon rind and juice.

Sift together the flour and baking powder. Gradually add the dry ingredients to the creamed mixture.

Shape the dough into a smooth ball, wrap it in wax paper and chill for at least 3 hours, or overnight.

Lightly grease baking sheets. Preheat the oven to 190°C (375°F).

The dough will be quite hard when it comes out of the refrigerator. Cut it into quarters and roll each quarter between pieces of wax paper until very thin. Cut with a cookie cutter and sprinkle with coloured sugar, if desired.

Bake for about 8 minutes, or until the cookies start to become golden around the edges. Cool on racks and store in an air-tight container.
Yields 7 dozen 5 cm (2″) cookies.

MAPLE-WALNUT COOKIES

Sugar was not refined in Canada until 1854. These delicious cookies come from those early days, when maple sugar was the only sweetener for many pioneer families.

250	mL butter	(1 cup)
250	mL grated or granular maple sugar	(1 cup)
250	mL firmly packed brown sugar	(1 cup)
2	eggs, well beaten	
5	mL vanilla	(1 tsp)
30	mL water	(2 Tbs)
750	mL all-purpose flour	(3 cups)
10	mL baking powder	(2 tsp)
250	mL finely chopped walnuts	(1 cup)

Cream the butter, add the maple sugar and brown sugar and beat until light and fluffy. Beat in the eggs. Stir in the vanilla and water.

Sift the flour and baking powder together and add gradually to the creamed mixture. Stir in the nuts. The dough will be quite soft. Wrap in wax paper and chill for 3 hours or longer.

Lightly grease baking sheets. Preheat the oven to 190°C (375°F).

Cut the dough into quarters and roll it out to a thickness of 3 mm (⅛") between two sheets of wax paper. Cut into the desired shapes with cookie cutters. Place 2 cm (¾") apart on sheets. Bake for 10 minutes, or until golden brown. Cool on racks and store in an air-tight container.

Yields about 11 dozen 5 cm (2") cookies.

SCOTCH BARS

This is a quick and delicious bar cookie that children can easily make.

125	mL butter	(½ cup)
50	mL granulated sugar	(¼ cup)
50	mL lightly packed brown sugar	(¼ cup)
1	egg	
5	mL vanilla	(1 tsp)
125	mL all-purpose flour	(½ cup)
125	mL rolled oats	(½ cup)
250	mL semi-sweet chocolate chips	(1 cup)
15	mL butter	(1 Tbs)
	chopped walnuts or coloured cocoanut	

Grease a 2.5 L (9"x9") tin. Preheat the oven to 180°C (350°F).

Cream the 125 mL butter, add the granulated sugar and brown sugar and beat until light and fluffy. Beat in the egg. Stir in the vanilla, flour and rolled oats.

Turn into the prepared pan and bake for 20 to 25 minutes, or until lightly browned. Remove from the oven and let cool for 10 minutes.

Meanwhile, melt the chocolate chips and the 15 mL butter together in the top of a double boiler. Spread over the baked bar and sprinkle immediately with chopped walnuts or coloured cocoanut. Cool. Cut into squares. Yields 36 squares.

LEMON BARS

The lemon in the icing provides a refreshing topping for this rich cookie.

Base

125 mL butter	(½ cup)
50 mL firmly packed brown sugar	(¼ cup)
250 mL all-purpose flour	(1 cup)

Second Layer:

250 mL finely chopped brazil nuts	(1 cup)
2 eggs, lightly beaten	
250 mL firmly packed brown sugar	(1 cup)
5 mL vanilla	(1 tsp)
15 mL cornstarch	(1 Tbs)
5 mL baking powder	(1 tsp)
1 mL salt	(¼ tsp)
250 mL chopped candied cherries	(1 cup)
125 mL shredded cocoanut	(½ cup)

Icing

45 mL butter	(3 Tbs)
500 mL icing sugar	(2 cups)
10 mL grated lemon rind	(2 tsp)
30 mL lemon juice	(2 Tbs)

Grease a 2.3 L (9"x11") pan. Preheat the oven to 180°C (350°F).

To make the base, cream the butter, gradually add the brown sugar and beat until light and fluffy. Stir in the flour. The mixture will be quite crumbly. Pat evenly into the prepared pan.

Bake for 8 to 10 minutes, or until light golden. Cool for 20 minutes before putting on the second layer.

Meanwhile, prepare the second layer. Mix together lightly the eggs, sugar and vanilla. Add the cornstarch, baking powder, salt, nuts, cherries and cocoanut and mix well. Pour over the base and bake for 35 to 40 minutes, or until fairly well set and light brown on top. Cool and ice.

To prepare the icing, cream the butter, gradually add the icing sugar and cream together until light and fluffy. Mix in the lemon juice and rind. Stir in a few drops of food colouring if you wish. Yellow will suggest the lemon flavour.

Cover and store in an air-tight container one day before cutting into small squares. Yields 4 dozen bars.

APRICOT BARS

Base

same ingredients as for Lemon Bars

Topping

200 mL dried apricots (packed into measure)	(¾ cup)
250 mL firmly packed brown sugar	(1 cup)
2 eggs	
75 mL all-purpose flour	(⅓ cup)
2 mL baking powder	(½ tsp)
1 mL salt	(¼ tsp)
5 mL grated orange rind	(1 tsp)
2 mL vanilla	(½ tsp)
125 mL chopped pecans	(½ cup)
icing sugar	

Grease a 2 L (8"x8") pan. Preheat the oven to 180°C (350°F).

To make the base, proceed as for Lemon Bars and bake at 180°C for 8 to 10 minutes, or until light golden. Cool for 20 minutes before putting on the topping.

To prepare the topping, rinse the apricots and place them in a saucepan with just enough water to cover. Bring them to a boil. Reduce the heat and simmer, uncovered, for 15 minutes, or until tender. Drain, cool and chop.

Beat the brown sugar and eggs together. Sift together the flour, baking powder and salt. Stir the dry ingredients into the brown sugar mixture. Add the orange rind, vanilla, pecans and apricots. Spread over the baked layer.

Bake for 30 minutes, or until the top is golden. Do not overbake.

Sprinkle the warm bars with icing sugar and cool before cutting. Store in an air-tight container.

Yields 36 tiny bars.

CHRISTMAS FRUIT BARS

These easy bars are a pleasant mixture of orange and date, topped with an interesting icing.

125	mL butter	(½ cup)
250	mL granulated sugar	(1 cup)
1	egg	
30	mL frozen orange juice concentrate	(2 Tbs)
10	mL grated orange rind	(2 tsp)
5	mL vanilla	(1 tsp)
300	mL all-purpose flour	(1¼ cups)
250	mL chopped dates	(1 cup)
125	mL chopped walnuts	(½ cup)
125	mL diced mixed candied fruit	(½ cup)
2	mL baking soda	(½ tsp)
1	mL salt	(¼ tsp)

Icing (optional)

30	mL butter	(2 Tbs)
250	mL icing sugar	(1 cup)
15	mL dark rum	(1 Tbs)
7	mL orange juice	(1½ tsp)
45	mL diced mixed candied fruit	(3 Tbs)

Grease and flour a 2.5 L (9" x 9") pan. Preheat the oven to 180°C (350°F).

To make the bars, cream the butter, add the sugar and beat until light and fluffy. Beat in the egg. Stir in the orange juice concentrate, orange rind and vanilla.

Combine 50 mL (¼ cup) of the flour with the fruit and nuts. Sift together the remaining flour, the soda and salt. Add the dry ingredients to the creamed mixture. Stir in the floured fruit and nuts.

Spread the batter evenly in the prepared pan. Bake for 30 minutes, or until a skewer inserted in the middle comes out clean.

Cool. Ice with the icing or cut into small squares and roll each in granulated sugar.

To make the icing, cream the butter and icing sugar together. Blend in the rum and orange juice and beat until smooth. Spread over the bars and decorate with candied fruit. Cut into small squares and store in an air-tight container.

Yields 64 small squares.

LIGHT ROLLED SHORTBREAD

250 mL butter	(1 cup)
125 mL icing sugar	(½ cup)
500 mL all-purpose flour	(2 cups)
decorating candies or chopped candied cherries	

Cream the butter thoroughly, add the sugar and beat until light and fluffy. Add the flour a bit at a time and mix well. Refrigerate the dough overnight.

Preheat the oven to 150°C (300°F).

Working with a small portion at a time, roll the dough out to a thickness of 6 mm (¼") between two pieces of wax paper. Cut into desired shapes with cookie cutters. Decorate with candies or pieces of cherries or simply prick with the tines of a fork three times.

Bake on ungreased baking sheets for 20 to 25 minutes, or until firm. Do not let the cookies brown on top. Cool on racks and store in an air-tight container.
Yields about 5 dozen cookies.

WHIPPED TENDER SHORTBREAD

250 mL soft butter	(1 cup)
125 mL icing sugar	(½ cup)
375 mL all-purpose flour	(1½ cups)
125 mL cornstarch	(½ cup)
coloured sugar decorating candies or chopped candied cherries	

Preheat the oven to 150°C (300°F).

Using an electric mixer, beat the butter until very fluffy. Slowly add the icing sugar and continue to beat until light and fluffy.

Sift together the flour and cornstarch. Add the dry ingredients very gradually to the creamed mixture, beating constantly.

Drop by small spoonfuls onto ungreased baking sheets and press each cookie slightly with the floured tines of a fork, or put the dough through a cookie press. Decorate the cookies with bits of cherry, coloured sugar and candies, if desired.

Bake for 30 minutes, or until set. Do not let the cookies brown on top.
Yields 4 dozen cookies.

COCOANUT MACAROONS

3 egg whites	
250 mL granulated sugar	(1 cup)
7 mL cornstarch	(1½ tsp)
500 mL shredded cocoanut	(2 cups)
5 mL vanilla	(1 tsp)

Lightly grease cookie sheets. Preheat the oven to 160°C (325°F).

In the top of a double boiler, beat the egg whites until stiff. Gradually beat in the sugar.

Cook over medium heat for about 5 minutes, beating constantly, until a crust forms on the bottom and sides of the pan. Remove from the heat.

Mix together the cornstarch, cocoanut and vanilla. Add to the egg white mixture. Blend well.

Drop the batter by small spoonfuls onto the prepared sheets. Bake for 12 minutes, or until light golden. Cool on racks and store in an air-tight container.
Yields 3½ dozen cookies.

Variations:

Cherry-Cocoanut Macaroons

Add 250 mL (1 cup) chopped red and green candied cherries when you mix in the cocoanut and vanilla and proceed as for Cocoanut Macaroons.

Chocolate Macaroons

Melt 1 square (1 oz) semi-sweet chocolate over hot water. Add when you add cocoanut and proceed as for Cocoanut Macaroons.

HOLIDAY BREADS AND SPREADS

INTRODUCTION

The recipes which follow reflect a variety of holiday breads and rolls, ranging from long-established Canadian favourites to the ethnic breads which recently have come to enrich our Christmas selection.

Notice that an approximate quantity is often given for the flour in yeast-bread recipes. There are many factors that affect the balance of liquid to dry ingredients, and sometimes the flour will absorb more liquid than others. There is one easy way to determine if enough flour has been added: when the dough is smooth and pliable and no longer sticky, there is no need to add more flour.

Let the yeast dough rise in a warm, draft-free place. One way to achieve even low heat is to put the container of dough on a heating pad, set at low.

All of the quick breads in this chapter freeze well and can be sliced as needed without thawing the whole loaf. Serve them buttered or with the spreads that are included at the end of this chapter, at lunch, dinner—or with breakfast!

LIGHT PUMPKIN LOAF

125	mL butter	(½ cup)
250	mL granulated sugar	(1 cup)
2	eggs	
250	mL pumpkin purée	(1 cup)
2	mL lemon extract	(½ tsp)
500	mL all-purpose flour	(2 cups)
10	mL baking powder	(2 tsp)
1	mL salt	(¼ tsp)
375	mL diced mixed candied fruit	(1½ cups)

Grease and flour a 2 L (9" x 5") loaf tin. Preheat the oven to 180°C (350°F).

Cream the butter, add the sugar and beat until light and fluffy. Add the eggs, one at a time, beating well after each addition. Stir in the pumpkin purée and lemon extract.

Use 30 mL (2 Tbs) of the flour to dredge the fruit. Sift together the remaining flour, baking powder and salt. Add the dry ingredients to the pumpkin mixture and quickly blend. Fold in the prepared fruit.

Turn into the prepared tin and bake for 1 hour and 20 minutes, or until a skewer inserted in the middle of the loaf comes out clean.

Cool in the tin for 10 minutes. Remove the loaf and cool completely on a rack. Wrap and store for a day before serving.

Cut in slices and butter. Serve it as an unusual Christmas cake or give it as a gift, along with a jar of Pumpkin Marmalade (see page 63).
Yields 1 loaf.

GLAZED CRANBERRY-LEMON LOAF

This refreshing holiday bread comes from British Columbia, where a large percentage of Canada's cranberries are grown.

50 mL	butter	(¼ cup)
175 mL	granulated sugar	(¾ cup)
2	eggs	
10 mL	grated lemon rind	(2 tsp)
500 mL	all-purpose flour	(2 cups)
250 mL	raw chopped cranberries	(1 cup)
125 mL	chopped walnuts	(½ cup)
125 mL	diced candied mixed peel	(½ cup)
12 mL	baking powder	(2½ tsp)
5 mL	salt	(1 tsp)
1 mL	cinnamon	(¼ tsp)
175 mL	milk	(¾ cup)
15 mL	lemon juice	(1 Tbs)
30 mL	granulated sugar	(2 Tbs)

Grease and flour a 2 L (9" x 5") loaf tin. Preheat the oven to 180°C (350°F).

Cream the butter, add the 175 mL sugar and beat until light and fluffy. Beat in the eggs, one at a time. Add the lemon rind.

Mix 50 mL (¼ cup) of the flour with the cranberries, walnuts and candied peel. Sift together the remaining flour, baking powder, salt and cinnamon. Add the dry ingredients alternately with the milk to the creamed mixture, beginning and ending with the dry ingredients. Stir only enough to mix.

Stir in the floured cranberries, walnuts and candied peel until all the ingredients are well distributed. Do not overmix.

Turn into the prepared tin and bake for 1 hour and 10 minutes, or until a skewer inserted in the middle of the loaf comes out clean. Cool in the tin for 5 minutes.

Meanwhile, combine the lemon juice and the 25 mL sugar. Drizzle the mixture over top of the loaf.

Let stand for 5 minutes longer. Remove from the pan and cool completely on a rack. Wrap and store for a day before serving. Yields 1 loaf.

GLAZED TANGERINE BREAD

	peel from 2 medium tangerines	
0.5 mL	salt	(⅛ tsp)
	cold water	
175 mL	granulated sugar	(¾ cup)
75 mL	water	(⅓ cup)
1	egg, well beaten	
75 mL	melted butter (measure before melting)	(⅓ cup)
175 mL	tangerine juice	(¾ cup)
500 mL	all-purpose flour	(2 cups)
10 mL	baking powder	(2 tsp)
5 mL	salt	(1 tsp)
150 mL	chopped dates	(⅔ cup)

Glaze

50 mL	icing sugar	(¼ cup)
30 mL	tangerine juice	(2 Tbs)
15 mL	grated tangerine peel	(1 Tbs)

Cover the peel from 2 tangerines with the salt and cold water and cook, uncovered, for about 20 minutes, until tender. Drain, rinse with cold water and drain again. Discard all the pith and chop the peel finely. Set aside.

Boil together for about 5 minutes the sugar and the 75 mL water. Add the cooked peel and simmer, uncovered, over medium-high heat for 5 minutes longer.

Grease and flour a 2 L (9" x 5") loaf tin. Preheat the oven to 180°C (350°F).

Beat together the egg, melted butter, the 175 mL tangerine juice and the peel and syrup mixture.

Sift together the flour, baking powder and salt and blend into this mixture. Fold in the dates. Do not overmix. Turn into the prepared tin and bake for 1 hour and 10 minutes, or until a skewer inserted in the middle of the loaf comes out clean. Let the bread sit in the tin for 5 minutes.

Meanwhile, prepare the glaze by combining the icing sugar, 30 mL tangerine juice and 15 mL tangerine peel. Pour over the loaf and let it sit 5 minutes longer. Remove the loaf from the tin and cool it completely on a rack. Wrap and store for a day before using. Yields 1 loaf.

CHERRY BREAD

125 mL butter	(½ cup)
250 mL granulated sugar	(1 cup)
2 eggs	
500 mL all-purpose flour	(2 cups)
15 mL baking powder	(1 Tbs)
2 mL salt	(½ tsp)
175 g maraschino cherries	(6 oz jar)
milk	
125 mL chopped walnuts	(½ cup)

Preheat the oven to 180°C (350°F). Grease and flour a 2 L (9" x 5") loaf tin.

Cream the butter, add the sugar and beat until light and fluffy. Beat in the eggs, one at a time.

Sift together the flour, baking powder and salt. Drain all the syrup from the maraschino cherries into a 250 mL (1 cup) measure. Fill to 250 mL with milk. Cut the cherries in half and dredge them and the walnuts with some of the flour mixture.

Add the rest of the dry ingredients to the creamed mixture, alternately with the cherry liquid. Stir in the floured cherries and walnuts, but do not overmix.

Turn into the prepared tin and bake for 1 hour and 10 minutes, or until a skewer inserted in the middle of the loaf comes out clean.

Cool in the pan for 10 minutes. Remove and cool completely on a rack. Wrap and store for a day before serving. Yields 1 loaf.

CANDIED FRUIT LOAF

50 mL butter	(¼ cup)
125 mL granulated sugar	(½ cup)
1 egg	
5 mL vanilla	(1 tsp)
175 mL diced mixed candied fruit	(¾ cup)
125 mL chopped walnuts	(½ cup)
500 mL all-purpose flour	(2 cups)
12 mL baking powder	(2½ tsp)
2 mL salt	(½ tsp)
2 mL baking soda	(½ tsp)
250 mL sour cream	(1 cup)
50 mL milk	(¼ cup)
10 mL grated orange rind	(2 tsp)

Grease and flour a 2 L (9" x 5") loaf tin. Preheat the oven to 180°C (350°F).

Cream the butter, add the sugar and beat until light and fluffy. Beat in the egg and add the vanilla.

Dredge the fruit and nuts in 50 mL (¼ cup) of the flour. Sift together the remaining flour, baking powder and salt. Stir the baking soda into the sour cream.

Add the dry ingredients alternately with the milk and the sour cream mixture to the creamed mixture, beginning and ending with the dry ingredients. Stir only enough to mix. Stir in the floured fruit and nuts and the orange rind.

Turn into the prepared tin and bake for 1 hour, or until a skewer inserted in the middle of the loaf comes out clean.

Cool in the pan for 10 minutes. Remove and cool completely on a rack. Wrap and store for a day before serving. Yields 1 loaf.

MINCEMEAT MUFFINS

Topping

30 mL	brown sugar	(2 Tbs)
15 mL	all-purpose flour	(1 Tbs)
2 mL	cinnamon	(½ tsp)
0.5 mL	ground cloves	(⅛ tsp)
10 mL	butter	(2 tsp)

Muffins

1	egg	
50 mL	granulated sugar	(¼ cup)
50 mL	vegetable oil	(¼ cup)
5 mL	vanilla	(1 tsp)
250 mL	milk	(1 cup)
175 mL	Mincemeat (see page 29)	(¾ cup)
250 mL	bran	(1 cup)
250 mL	all-purpose flour	(1 cup)
10 mL	baking powder	(2 tsp)
2 mL	salt	(½ tsp)
125 mL	coarsely chopped walnuts	(½ cup)

Grease 15 muffin cups. Preheat the oven to 180°C (350°F).

To prepare the topping, combine the brown sugar, flour and spices. Cut in the butter until the mixture resembles rolled oats. Set aside.

To prepare the muffin batter, beat the egg and sugar together. Stir in the oil, vanilla, milk, mincemeat and bran. Sift the flour, baking powder and salt together and add the dry ingredients to the mincemeat mixture. Stir in the walnuts.

Fill the prepared muffin cups three-quarters full, sprinkle with the prepared topping and bake for 30 minutes, or until a skewer inserted in the centre of a muffin comes out clean. Yields 15 medium muffins.

SNOW MUFFINS

During the Christmas holidays, have some fun with your children and make these magic muffins. Have all the other ingredients at hand, and just before you need it, collect the snow. Spoon it into the measuring cup–do not pack it in–then work quickly.

45 mL	butter	(3 Tbs)
500 mL	all-purpose flour	(2 cups)
250 mL	lightly packed brown sugar	(1 cup)
15 mL	baking powder	(1 Tbs)
5 mL	salt	(1 tsp)
250 mL	milk	(1 cup)
375 mL	clean white snow	(1½ cups)
175 mL	currants or raisins	(¾ cup)

Grease 12 medium-sized muffin cups. Preheat the oven to 190°C (375°F).

Measure the butter and melt it over low heat in a small pan.

Mix together the flour, brown sugar, baking powder and salt. Add the melted butter and milk. Don't worry if the mixture is lumpy. Quickly mix in the snow and currants or raisins, stirring only to blend.

Spoon into muffin cups and bake for 20 to 25 minutes, or until light brown.
Yields 12 medium muffins.

DINNER ROLLS

Since these delicate white rolls freeze very well, you can have them on hand for special holiday meals.

25	mL granulated sugar	(2 Tbs)
125	mL lukewarm water	(½ cup)
2	envelopes active dry yeast	
250	mL buttermilk or sour milk	(1 cup)
5	mL salt	(1 tsp)
50	mL granulated sugar	(¼ cup)
50	mL shortening, softened	(¼ cup)
1-1.25	L all-purpose flour	(4-5 cups)
2	mL baking soda	(½ tsp)
1	egg, beaten	

Dissolve the 25 mL sugar in the lukewarm water, sprinkle on the yeast and set aside for 10 minutes.

Pour the buttermilk into a large bowl and add the salt, 50 mL sugar and shortening. Stir in 250 mL (1 cup) of the flour. Stir the yeast mixture briskly and add to the first mixture. Then add the baking soda and egg and mix well.

Mix in enough of the remaining flour to produce a smooth dough. Turn out onto a lightly floured board and knead for 5 minutes, or until smooth and elastic. Place in a greased bowl, cover with greased wax paper and a towel, and let rise in a warm place for about 1 hour and 45 minutes, or until the dough is double in bulk.

Punch down the dough. Shape into rolls and place them 8 cm (3") apart on a greased baking sheet. Grease the top of the buns and let rise for about 45 minutes, or until double in size.

Preheat the oven to 190°C (375°F) and bake the rolls for 10 to 12 minutes, or until golden brown and hollow sounding when the bottoms are tapped. Remove to racks and cool.

Yields 2 dozen 6 cm (2½") rolls.

STOLLEN

Stollen is a heavy German fruit bread that takes its name from its shape. "Stollen" means sticks or posts and once symbolized the Christ Child in the crèche.

1.375-1.5L	all-purpose flour	(5½-6 cups)
125	mL seedless raisins	(½ cup)
125	mL currants	(½ cup)
75	mL finely chopped candied citron	(⅓ cup)
	or	
50	mL finely diced angelica	(¼ cup)
250	mL diced mixed candied peel	(1 cup)
125	mL halved candied cherries	(½ cup)
250	mL blanched slivered almonds	(1 cup)
300	mL milk	(1¼ cups)
125	mL butter	(½ cup)
125	mL granulated sugar	(½ cup)
5	mL salt	(1 tsp)
10	mL granulated sugar	(2 tsp)
125	mL lukewarm water (43°C)	(½ cup at 110°F)
2	envelopes active dry yeast	
2	mL almond extract	(½ tsp)
5	mL grated lemon rind	(1 tsp)
2	eggs, slightly beaten	
50-75	mL melted butter	(¼-⅓ cup)
50	mL icing sugar	(¼ cup)

Sprinkle 50 mL (¼ cup) of the flour over the raisins, currants, citron or angelica, candied peel, cherries and almonds. Set aside.

Scald the milk, pour it into a large bowl and add the 125 mL butter, 125 mL sugar and salt. Stir until the butter melts.

Meanwhile, dissolve the 10 mL sugar in the lukewarm water in a large bowl. Sprinkle the dry yeast over it. Set aside for 10 minutes, then stir briskly and add to the milk mixture. Stir in the almond flavouring, lemon rind and eggs.

Add 750 mL (3 cups) of the flour and beat until smooth. Gradually add enough of the remaining flour to make a stiff dough that leaves the sides of the bowl.

Turn the dough out onto a floured board and knead for 10 minutes, or until the dough is smooth and elastic. Press the floured fruit and nuts into the dough a bit at a time. Do not handle the dough too much at this point or the bread will be discoloured.

Grease a large bowl with some of the melted butter and place the dough in it. Cover with greased wax paper and a towel and let rise in a warm place for 2 hours, or until double in bulk.

Punch down the dough and divide it into two pieces. Let the dough rest for 10 minutes, then roll the two pieces into strips about 30 cm (12") long, 20 cm (8") wide and 1 cm (½") thick. Brush each with 30 mL (2 Tbs) of the melted butter and sprinkle each with 25 mL (2 Tbs) of the icing sugar. Bring one long side of each strip over to the centre of the strip and press the edge down. Then fold the other long side across it, overlapping the seam down the centre by about 2 cm (1"). Shape the loaf gently with your hands so that it mounds in the centre.

Grease two baking sheets, place the loaves on them and brush them with the rest of the melted butter. Let the bread rise in a warm place for about 1 hour, or until doubled in volume.

Preheat the oven to 190°C (375°F). Bake the bread for 45 minutes, or until golden brown and crusty. Transfer the loaves to racks to cool completely. Just before serving, sprinkle with additional icing sugar.

Yields two 30 cm x 10 cm (12" x 4") loaves.

Note: Stollen is traditionally served with a generous sprinkling of icing sugar, but if you prefer an icing glaze for the top, use the following.

175	mL icing sugar	(¾ cup)
15	mL milk	(1 Tbs)
1	mL almond extract	(¼ tsp)

Combine all of the ingredients in a small bowl. Beat until smooth and spread on the hot bread. If you wish, sprinkle a few spoonfuls of diced candied peel or fruit on top for garnish.

BEIGNES

(Old-Fashioned Doughnuts)

Over the years, most Canadian cookbooks and private recipe collections have contained at least one doughnut recipe. These "fried cakes", as they were once called, are still a favourite holiday dessert in French-Canadian homes.

30	mL butter	(2 Tbs)
375	mL granulated sugar	(1½ cups)
2	eggs, beaten	
750	mL all-purpose flour	(3 cups)
5	mL baking soda	(1 tsp)
5	mL cream of tartar	(1 tsp)
10	mL salt	(2 tsp)
3	mL freshly grated nutmeg	(¾ tsp)
2	mL ground ginger	(½ tsp)
250	mL milk	(1 cup)
250	mL all-purpose flour	(1 cup)
	vegetable oil or shortening for deep frying	
	pinch of ginger	
	icing sugar	

Cream the butter, add the sugar and eggs and beat together until light and fluffy.

Sift together the 750 mL flour, baking soda, cream of tartar, salt and spices. Stir the dry ingredients into the creamed mixture alternately with the milk.

Spread the 250 mL flour on a board. Gently knead the dough, incorporating only enough flour to prevent the dough from sticking (the less flour, the better).

Wrap and refrigerate for 3 hours or longer.

Heat the oil or shortening to 190°C (375°F). Put a pinch of ginger in the oil to prevent the oil from soaking into the doughnuts. Take care to maintain the oil at a constant temperature during the frying process.

Roll out the chilled dough in sections on a lightly floured board to a thickness of 8 mm (⅓"). Cut with a doughnut cutter. Using a slotted spoon, carefully place the doughnuts in the fat. Turning only once, fry the doughnuts for 3 to 5 minutes, until golden brown on both sides. Don't put too many doughnuts in the oil at the same time. Lift each doughnut carefully from the oil with the slotted spoon. Drain thoroughly on paper towelling. Cool and sprinkle generously with icing sugar.

Don't forget to fry the holes! Kids love these.

Doughnuts keep well. To revive the just-cooked flavour, simply place them in a pan and heat, uncovered, in a 180°C (350°F) oven for a few minutes.

Yields 30 doughnuts or 24 doughnuts and 24 holes.

BUTTER KRINGLE

Kringle is a Danish Christmas bread, traditionally made in the form of a pretzel. The pretzel shape derived from a pagan calendar symbol marking the winter solstice—a circle representing the sun's course, with a dot in the centre representing the earth. This Icelandic version of Butter Kringle from Manitoba is made simply in long loaves, but in other ways it is identical to the Danish Bread.

250	mL milk	(1 cup)
35	mL lard	(2½ Tbs)
25	mL granulated sugar	(2 Tbs)
5	mL granulated sugar	(1 tsp)
125	mL lukewarm water	(½ cup)
2	envelopes active dry yeast	
625-750	mL all-purpose flour	(2½-3 cups)
250	mL softened butter	(1 cup)

Filling

175	mL boiling water	(¾ cup)
175	mL chopped seedless raisins	(¾ cup)
250	mL brown sugar	(1 cup)
175	mL chopped pecans	(¾ cup)
2	mL ground cardamom	(½ tsp)

Topping

1	slightly beaten egg	
50	mL granulated sugar	(¼ cup)
50	mL blanched sliced almonds	(¼ cup)

Scald the milk and put it in a large bowl with the lard and the 25 mL sugar.

Meanwhile, dissolve the 5 mL sugar in the lukewarm water, sprinkle the yeast on top and let stand for 10 minutes. When the yeast bubbles up and increases in volume, stir briskly and add to the milk mixture.

Add 375 mL (1½ cups) of the flour to the yeast and milk mixture and beat until very smooth. Beat in enough of the remaining 375 mL (1½ cups) of flour to make a dough which leaves the sides of the bowl. Chill for one hour in a greased bowl covered loosely with greased wax paper. The dough will rise in the refrigerator.

Turn onto a floured board and roll into a thin rectangle, approximately 30 cm x 40 cm (12" x 16"). Spread a quarter of the softened butter over half the dough. Cover with the other half of the dough and roll again, pounding the dough with the rolling pin. Place on a greased baking sheet, cover loosely with greased wax paper and refrigerate for 1 hour. Once again, roll the dough into a rectangle, spread half with butter, cover with the other half of the dough, pound and chill. Repeat this process four times in all.

After the last hour of chilling, roll the dough into a thin rectangle, approximately 30 cm x 40 cm (12" x 16"), and cut into three long strips.

Prepare the filling and topping while the dough is being processed.

To make the filling, boil the water, add the raisins and bring to a boil again. Pour off the water and drain raisins thoroughly. Dry on a paper towel. Mix raisins with the brown sugar, pecans and cardamom.

Place a third of the raisin and sugar mixture along the middle of each strip of dough. Fold the edges over to meet and seal all edges well. Chill at least overnight, wrapped loosely in greased wax paper.

When you wish to bake the bread, preheat the oven to 220°C (425°F). Place the loaves on greased baking sheets, leaving plenty of room for expansion.

For the topping, brush the loaves with the beaten egg. Mix together the granulated sugar and almonds. Sprinkle on the top of the loaves. Bake for 20 to 25 minutes, or until browned on top. Serve warm.

Kringle can be made well ahead of time and frozen. Reheat the loaves in foil in a 190°C (375°F) oven for about 20 minutes. There is no need to thaw the loaves before heating.

Yields 3 loaves.

CHELSEA BUNS

Chelsea Buns have been popular across Canada for many years. These very delicious ones would be a treat for any holiday breakfast.

250	mL milk	(1 cup)
75	mL granulated sugar	(⅓ cup)
10	mL salt	(2 tsp)
125	mL shortening	(½ cup)
125	mL water	(½ cup)
5	mL sugar	(1 tsp)
125	mL lukewarm water	(½ cup)
1	envelope active dry yeast	
1.25	L all-purpose flour	(5 cups)
175	mL lightly packed brown sugar	(¾ cup)
45	mL butter	(3 Tbs)
45	mL hot water	(3 Tbs)
175	mL red and green maraschino cherries	(¾ cup)
250	mL seedless raisins	(1 cup)
125	mL pecan halves	(½ cup)
125	mL soft butter	(½ cup)
175	mL lightly packed brown sugar	(¾ cup)
15	mL cinnamon	(1 Tbs)

Scald the milk. Pour it into a large bowl and add the 75 mL sugar, salt, shortening and the first 125 mL water. Stir until the shortening melts. Cool to lukewarm.

Meanwhile, dissolve the 5 mL sugar in the lukewarm water. Sprinkle the yeast over the water and let sit for 10 minutes, then stir briskly and add to the milk mixture. Beat in 625 mL (2½ cups) of the flour. Then gradually add enough of the remaining flour to make a soft dough.

Turn the dough onto a floured board and knead for 8 to 10 minutes, or until the dough is smooth and elastic. Shape into a ball. Grease a bowl and place the dough in it, rolling the ball to grease the entire surface. Cover with greased wax paper and a damp cloth and let rise in a warm place for about 1½ hours, or until doubled in bulk.

Punch down the dough, knead two or three times and let rest for 10 minutes on a board.

Meanwhile, prepare a syrup for the buns. Put the first 175 mL brown sugar, 45 mL butter and 45 mL hot water in a pan. Stir over medium heat until the butter melts, then boil for 2 minutes. Immediately pour into two greased 1.5-2 L (10") round pans.

Drain the cherries thoroughly and cut them into halves. Divide the cherries, raisins and pecans between the two pans, sprinkling them evenly over the bottoms.

Roll the dough into a 22.5 cm x 35 cm (9" x 14") rectangle. Spread with the soft butter. Sprinkle with the last 175 mL brown sugar and the cinnamon. Roll up from the long side into a tight roll. Cut into 16 even pieces and place the pieces, cut side down, in the prepared pans. Grease the tops, cover with greased wax paper and a damp towel and let rise in a warm place for about 45 minutes, or until double in bulk.

Preheat the oven to 190°C (375°F). Bake the buns for 25 minutes, or until golden brown. Place strips of wax paper under a rack. As soon as the buns come out of the oven, turn the pans upside down on rack. Allow the syrup to run over the buns and remove the pans.

Yields 16 buns.

BUBBLE BREAD

Serve this unusual bread as a special Christmas morning breakfast with fresh fruit, a creamy cheese and coffee.

250	mL milk	(1 cup)
50	mL butter	(¼ cup)
5	mL salt	(1 tsp)
50	mL granulated sugar	(¼ cup)
5	mL granulated sugar	(1 tsp)
50	mL lukewarm water	(¼ cup)
1	envelope active dry yeast	
1	egg, slightly beaten	
875	mL-1L all-purpose flour	(3½-4 cups)
50	mL red or green candied cherries	(¼ cup)
150	mL melted butter	(⅔ cup)
175	mL chopped walnuts or pecans	(¾ cup)
45	mL melted butter	(3 Tbs)
125	mL corn syrup	(½ cup)
5	mL vanilla	(1 tsp)

Scald the milk. Pour into a large bowl and add the butter, salt and the 50 mL granulated sugar. Stir to dissolve the sugar and melt the butter.

Meanwhile, dissolve the 5 mL sugar in the lukewarm water. Sprinkle the yeast over the water and let sit for 10 minutes, then stir briskly and add to the milk mixture. Stir in the egg. Gradually add about 875 mL (3½ cups) of the flour. Beat together well. Flour a board with the remaining flour and turn the dough out onto it. Knead the dough, incorporating only as much flour as necessary to keep the dough from sticking. Knead for 8 to 10 minutes, or until smooth and elastic.

Grease a large bowl. Place the dough in it, rolling it to grease the entire surface. Cover with greased wax paper and a damp towel and let rise in a warm place for about 2 hours, until double in volume.

Punch down the dough, turn out onto a lightly floured board, knead a few times and let rest for 10 minutes.

Meanwhile, grease a 3 L (10") tube pan with butter. Arrange the cherries on the bottom. Pinch off bits of dough and roll with hands into balls 2.5 cm (1") in diameter. Place a layer of balls in the prepared pan, about 1 cm (½ ") apart. Pour over these about a third of the 150 mL melted butter and a third of the nuts. Repeat with layers of balls of dough, butter and nuts until all the dough, nuts and butter are used. (If desired, more cherries may be placed between the layers of dough.) Cover as before and let rise in a warm place for about 45 minutes, until double in volume.

Preheat the oven to 180°C (350°F). Bake the bread for 35 to 40 minutes, or until it sounds hollow when tapped.

Mix together the 45 mL melted butter, corn syrup and vanilla. Very carefully pour over the top of the hot bread. Let sit in pan for 15 minutes. Place a piece of wax paper under a rack. Invert the pan over the rack and remove the pan.

Serve hot by breaking off balls of bread in individual servings.

If you wish to make Bubble Bread ahead of time, wrap the cooled bread in foil and reheat before serving. The bread will keep well for a day or two and will freeze well.
Yields 12 servings.

MAKIVNYK

(Poppy Seed Bread)

At "Svyata Vechera" (Christmas Eve dinner), Ukrainian Canadians enjoy a wide variety of breads and pastries. Very often Makivnyk, a sweet bread with poppy seed filling, is on the menu.

Filling

500	mL fresh poppy seeds	(2 cups)
	boiling water	
125	mL granulated sugar	(½ cup)
10	mL grated lemon rind	(2 tsp)
2	mL cinnamon	(½ tsp)
2	egg whites, stiffly beaten	
1	egg white, stiffly beaten	

Dough

500	mL milk	(2 cups)
5	mL granulated sugar	(1 tsp)
125	mL lukewarm water	(½ cup)
1	envelope active dry yeast	
125	mL butter	(½ cup)
125	mL granulated sugar	(½ cup)
5	mL salt	(1 tsp)
2	whole eggs	
2	egg yolks	
5	mL vanilla	(1 tsp)
7	mL grated lemon rind	(1½ tsp)
2.125	L all-purpose flour (approximately)	(8½ cups)
1	egg, well beaten	
15	mL water	(1 Tbs)

To make the filling, cover the poppy seeds with boiling water and soak for one hour. Drain and dry thoroughly. Grind with a food grinder fitted with a very fine blade.

Mix together the sugar, lemon rind, cinnamon and the 2 stiff egg whites. Mix gently with the ground poppy seed. Set aside.

To prepare the dough, scald the milk, then pour it into a large bowl and cool to lukewarm.

Meanwhile, dissolve the 5 mL sugar in the lukewarm water. Sprinkle yeast over the water and set aside for 10 minutes.

Add the butter, the 125 mL granulated sugar and the salt to the warm milk. Stir to melt the butter and dissolve the sugar.

Beat the eggs and yolks well. Add the eggs, vanilla and lemon rind to the milk. Stir the yeast mixture briskly and add to the milk mixture.

Add 1 L (4 cups) of the flour and beat thoroughly. Then gradually add enough of the remaining flour to make a soft dough that leaves the sides of the bowl. Turn out onto a floured board and knead for 8 to 10 minutes, or until the dough is smooth and elastic.

Grease a large bowl. Shape dough into a ball and place it in the bowl, rolling the ball to grease entire surface. Cover with greased wax paper and a damp towel and let rise in a warm place for about 1½ hours, until double in bulk.

Punch down the dough when it has risen and divide it into three equal parts. Roll each into a rectangle about 6 mm (¼") thick. Brush each rectangle with the remaining stiffly beaten egg white to keep the filling from separating from the dough.

Spread a third of the poppy seed filling over each rectangle. Starting from the long side, roll like a jelly roll and seal the edges by pinching together firmly. Place the rolls seam down on a greased baking sheet, leaving plenty of room for the dough to expand. Cover as before and let rise for about 45 minutes, or until double in volume.

(Sometimes the loaves are bent into horseshoe shapes or placed in greased 2 L [9" x 5"] loaf tins.)

Preheat the oven to 180°C (350°F).

Combine the beaten egg and water and brush the tops of the loaves with this mixture. Bake for about 45 minutes, or until golden brown and hollow sounding when tapped.

Cool on racks before cutting.
Yields 3 large loaves.

HERB BATTER BREAD

Quick and easy to make, this subtle herb bread goes very well with cold turkey or chicken.

1	envelope active dry yeast	
50	mL lukewarm water	(¼ cup)
175	mL milk	(¾ cup)
15	mL granulated sugar	(1 Tbs)
15	mL vegetable oil	(1 Tbs)
5	mL salt	(1 tsp)
5	mL dried crushed marjoram leaves	(1 tsp)
3	mL dried crushed thyme	(¾ tsp)
2	mL dry mustard	(½ tsp)
2	mL dried crushed dill weed	(½ tsp)
1	egg	
750	mL all-purpose flour	(3 cups)
	vegetable oil	
	milk	
	poppy seeds	

Sprinkle the yeast on lukewarm water in a large bowl. Let stand to soften, then stir briskly to dissolve. Scald the milk, then cool to lukewarm. Add the milk, sugar, oil, salt, marjoram, thyme, dry mustard, dill weed, egg and 500 mL (2 cups) of the flour to the yeast mixture. Beat at high speed with electric mixer for 3 minutes (or 10 minutes by hand). Stir in the remaining flour. Cover with greased wax paper and a damp towel and let rise in a warm place for about 1 hour, or until double in bulk.

Punch down the dough. Turn out onto a lightly floured board. Knead about 20 times. Place the dough in greased 2 L (9" x 5") loaf tin, making sure the dough fills the corners. Brush the top with oil. Cover as before and place in a warm place to rise for about 45 minutes, or until double in volume.

Preheat the oven to 190°C (375°F).

Brush the top of loaf with milk and sprinkle with poppy seeds. Bake for 40-50 minutes, or until golden brown and hollow sounding when tapped on top. Remove immediately from the pan and cool on a rack. Yields 1 loaf.

ORANGE SPREAD

Great with Candied Fruit Bread, Cranberry Loaf, Tangerine Loaf, muffins or toast.

50	mL butter	(¼ cup)
30	mL cream cheese	(2 Tbs)
50	mL icing sugar	(¼ cup)
30	mL grated orange rind	(2 Tbs)

Cream the butter and cream cheese together well. Add the icing sugar and beat until light and fluffy. Blend in the orange rind. Yields about 125 mL (½ cup) spread.

GINGER-NUT SPREAD

Spread on Light Pumpkin Loaf, Snow Muffins, Mincemeat Muffins or toast. Or fill cooked pear halves for use as garnish with meat and salad plates.

115	g cream cheese	(4 oz)
30	mL finely chopped candied ginger	(2 Tbs)
30	mL finely chopped pecans or walnuts	(2 Tbs)

Cream the cream cheese until light and fluffy. Blend in the ginger and nuts. Yields about 125 mL (½ cup) spread.

CHERRY-NUT SPREAD

Use as spread for Cherry Bread or Mincemeat Muffins.

115	g cream cheese	(4 oz)
30	mL finely diced red and green maraschino cherries	(2 Tbs)
30	mL finely chopped walnuts	(2 Tbs)
1	mL cherry extract	(¼ tsp)

Beat the cream cheese until light and fluffy. Drain the cherries thoroughly and blend into the cream cheese, along with the walnuts and cherry extract.

Yields about 125 mL (½ cup) spread.

PUMPKIN MARMALADE

Pumpkin Marmalade is a genuine treat and a convenient way to make use of pumpkins from the fall harvest long after the rush of fall preserving.

3.5	L cubed pumpkin or 1 medium-large pumpkin	(14 cups)
2	L granulated sugar	(8 cups)
3	oranges	
3	lemons	

Remove the rind and seeds from the pumpkin. Cut the flesh into 1 cm (½″) cubes. Mix the pumpkin and sugar together in a large preserving kettle. Stir well to dissolve the sugar. Cover and let sit overnight.

Next morning, remove the pumpkin from the juice with a slotted spoon and set aside. Cook the pot of juice over high heat. Bring to a boil, then reduce the heat to medium-high and boil gently, uncovered, for 20 minutes to reduce the liquid.

Meanwhile, remove the thin outer rind (zest) of the oranges and lemons, and set the zest aside. Remove all the bitter white membrane underneath and discard. Grind the zest and fruits in a grinder with a medium blade, or in a food processor fitted with a steel blade. Add the pumpkin, citrus fruits and rind to the boiling juice. Gently boil everything together for 1½ to 2 hours, uncovered, until the marmalade thickens and the pumpkin is translucent. The marmalade will be a rich golden-brown colour. Stir very frequently, especially near the end of the cooking time.

Remove from the heat. Let the marmalade cool very slightly while you skim off any foam from the top with a metal spoon. (This will prevent the fruit from floating to the tops of the jars.)

Ladle into hot sterilized jars and seal with a thin layer of melted wax.

Yields ten 225 g (8 oz) jars.

WINTER APRICOT CONSERVE

This tart yet sweet spread makes a tasty
Christmas gift.

500	g dried apricots	(1 lb)
875	mL cold water	(3½ cups)
175	g jar red maraschino cherries	(6 oz)
625	mL undrained crushed pineapple	(2½ cups)
25	mL grated lemon rind	(4 tsp)
75	mL lemon juice	(⅓ cup)
250	mL seedless sultana raisins	(1 cup)
1.5	L granulated sugar	(6 cups)

Cut the apricots into small pieces with
scissors, or use a food processor fitted with a
steel blade. Place the apricots in a large heavy
saucepan, cover with cold water and soak
overnight.

Next morning, drain the maraschino
cherries and reserve the juice. Cut cherries
into quarters with scissors and set aside.

Cook the apricots in the water in which
they were soaked, uncovered, for about 15
minutes, or until tender. Add the crushed
pineapple and pineapple juice, the grated
rind and lemon juice, raisins, maraschino
cherry juice and sugar. Cook uncovered over
medium heat, stirring often, for about 1½
hours, or until thick and clear.

Add the cherries and cook for 10 minutes
longer. Pour into hot sterilized jars and cover
with a thin layer of melted wax.
Yields about nine 225 g (8 oz) jars.

POTTED CHEESE

This sharp cheese spread should be prepared
a week in advance so that the flavours will
mingle. It will keep for weeks in the
refrigerator, but allow it to come to room
temperature for better spreading and taste.

225	g old cheddar cheese	(8 oz)
0.5	mL onion salt	(⅛ tsp)
3	mL dry mustard	(¾ tsp)
115	g cream cheese, softened	(4 oz)
	few drops red pepper sauce	
50	mL dry sherry	(¼ cup)

Shred the cheddar cheese finely. (If possible,
use a food processor for the shredding and
blending. The spread will be extra smooth
and creamy.) Add the onion salt and dry
mustard and mix well. Work in the cream
cheese. Add the pepper sauce and dry sherry.
Beat everything together until the mixture is
smooth and creamy.

Pack in a cheese crock and store in
refrigerator to serve with crackers or melba
toast.
Yields about 750 mL (3 cups) spread.

CANDY

INTRODUCTION

As soon as sugar became available in the nineteenth century, candy was made as an extremely special treat both for holiday eating and for decorating the Christmas tree. Today, it is an indispensable part of the Christmas tradition

Although candy-making demands accuracy and care, it need not be a difficult, mysterious operation. Here are some tips which will help make the experience both easy and enjoyable.

Temperature
Forget the fact that your grandmother made countless batches of perfect fudge without the aid of a thermometer and invest in one. Sugar passes through a number of definite stages when it is heated, and the temperature and cooking time are important factors in the success of the finished product.

Cooking Pans
Always use a large, heavy-bottomed saucepan for candy, since sugar burns easily and expands greatly when it boils. Buttering or oiling the saucepan will help keep the mixture from sticking.

Preparing the Candy
It is important to follow instructions for stirring the syrup. Stirring at the wrong stage will affect the texture of the finished product.

Even if you have never made candy before, by following the recipes closely and using a candy thermometer you will soon have dozens of homemade treats for your family and friends to enjoy.

CREAMY CHOCOLATE FUDGE

2	squares unsweetened chocolate	(2 oz)
500	mL granulated sugar	(2 cups)
150	mL evaporated milk or thin cream	(⅔ cup)
30	mL corn syrup	(2 Tbs)
45	mL butter	(3 Tbs)
5	mL vanilla	(1 tsp)

Grease a 2 L (8" x 8") square pan with butter.

Grease a heavy-bottomed saucepan with butter. Grate the chocolate into it and add the sugar, milk and corn syrup. Stir over low heat until chocolate melts and sugar dissolves. Increase the heat to medium-high and boil the mixture until it reaches soft ball stage (115°C or 240°F). Stir just enough to prevent scorching. Remove from the heat and add the butter. Cool to lukewarm (43°C or 110°F) without stirring. Add the vanilla.

Beat until the candy loses its gloss and becomes thick enough to hold its shape. This will take 10 minutes if you use a heavy electric mixer and longer by hand. Immediately pat into the prepared pan. Cool and cut into squares.
Yields 36 pieces.

MAPLE CREAM FUDGE

1 L lightly packed brown sugar	(4 cups)
30 mL all-purpose flour	(2 Tbs)
10 mL baking powder	(2 Tsp)
0.5 mL salt	(⅛ tsp)
250 mL thin cream or evaporated milk	(1 cup)
50 mL butter	(¼ cup)
5 mL vanilla	(1 tsp)

Grease a 2 L (8"x8") pan with butter for the finished fudge.

Lightly oil a large, heavy-bottomed saucepan. In it combine the brown sugar, flour, baking powder, salt and cream. Bring to the boiling point over medium heat, stirring until the sugar dissolves. Continue cooking until the mixture reaches the soft ball stage (115°C or 240°F), stirring only enough to prevent scorching.

Remove from the heat and add the butter. Then, without stirring, cool until lukewarm (43°C or 110°F). Add the vanilla and beat until the mixture is thick and loses its gloss.

Pour into pan and score into small squares when almost cool. If the fudge becomes too stiff before it is poured into pan, knead it until it softens, then press it into the pan or shape it into a roll and slice. If it doesn't set, stir in 50 mL (¼ cup) milk. Reheat to given temperature. Beat it again until it reaches the right consistency.
Yields 36 pieces.

WHITE CHRISTMAS FUDGE

750 mL granulated sugar	(3 cups)
250 mL corn syrup	(1 cup)
375 mL light cream	(1½ cups)
7 mL vanilla	(1½ tsp)
175 mL pecan halves	(¾ cup)
175 mL chopped walnuts	(¾ cup)
250 mL diced red and green candied cherries	(1 cup)
250 mL diced candied pineapple	(1 cup)

Grease a 2 L (8"x8") pan with butter for the finished fudge.

Lightly oil a large, heavy-bottomed saucepan. In it, combine the sugar, corn syrup and cream. Cook over low heat, stirring until the sugar is dissolved. Increase the heat to moderate and heat to boiling, stirring occasionally. Cook, without stirring, until the mixture reaches the soft ball stage (115°C or 240°F). Remove from the heat. Beat immediately until it begins to lose its gloss and starts to get stiff. Add the vanilla. Slowly stir in the nuts and fruit. Pack into the prepared pan and chill. Cut into small squares when cool.

This delicious fudge will keep soft for weeks if stored in an air-tight container in a cool place.
Yields 36 pieces.

TOFFEE

125 mL water	(½ cup)
500 mL lightly packed brown sugar	(2 cups)
500 mL molasses	(2 cups)
15 mL butter	(1 Tbs)
30 mL vinegar	(2 Tbs)
2 mL baking soda	(½ tsp)

Grease a baking sheet with butter.

Bring the water to a boil in a saucepan. Stir in the brown sugar, molasses, butter and vinegar. Boil the mixture, without stirring, until it reaches the hard ball stage (127°C or

260°F). Add the baking soda and mix well. Remove from the heat.

Pour onto the prepared sheet. With a metal spatula, fold the edges of the toffee towards the centre. Repeat several times until the mixture is cool enough to be pulled by hand. (This step takes a while.)

Thoroughly grease your hands with butter. Pull and stretch toffee over and over again. Work quickly because the toffee hardens very fast. (It's fun to let the children help you with this part.) The toffee will become lighter in colour as it hardens.

When it is too hard to pull, place the toffee on a baking sheet and roll into a thin slab.

Grease scissors or a knife with butter and cut the stick of toffee into 4 cm (1½") pieces. Wrap each piece in wax paper. Yields about 1 kg (2 lbs) toffee.

PEANUT BRITTLE

500	mL granulated sugar	(2 cups)
250	mL corn syrup	(1 cup)
250	mL water	(1 cup)
500	mL peanuts	(2 cups)
30	mL butter	(2 Tbs)
3	mL baking soda	(¾ tsp)

Lightly oil two baking sheets.

Combine the sugar, corn syrup and water in a large heavy saucepan. Stirring constantly, heat until the sugar dissolves. Then, stirring frequently, cook to the soft ball stage (115°C or 240°F). Continue cooking over medium-high heat, without stirring, until the mixture reaches the soft crack stage (137°C or 280°F). Stir in the peanuts and butter. Continue cooking to the hard crack stage (149°C or 300°F), stirring occasionally.

Remove from the heat, immediately stir in the baking soda and mix thoroughly. Quickly pour the candy onto the prepared sheets. As the candy cools, stretch it out by lifting and pulling the edges. Loosen from the sheets as soon as possible and turn the candy over. When it cools, break it into chunks. Yields about 1 kg (2¼ lbs) peanut brittle.

Variation:

Cocoanut-Orange Brittle

Substitute 375 mL (1½ cups) shredded cocoanut and 7 mL (1½ tsp) grated orange rind for the peanuts and proceed as for Peanut Brittle.

FILLED DATES

125	mL Almond Paste (see page 22)	(½ cup)
15	mL dark rum	(1 Tbs)
250	mL icing sugar	(1 cup)
45	mL finely chopped walnuts	(3 Tbs)
30	mL finely chopped dried apricots	(2 Tbs)
5	mL finely chopped crystallized ginger	(1 tsp)
	about 1 kg loosely packed pitted dates	(2 lbs)
	granulated sugar or unsweetened chocolate	

Moisten the almond paste with the rum. Gradually blend in the icing sugar. Stir in the walnuts, apricots and ginger.

Shape the paste into small bars and fill the dates. Roll the dates in granulated sugar or dip in melted chocolate. Yields about 5 dozen filled dates.

GLAZED ALMONDS

30 mL butter	(2 Tbs)
15 mL corn syrup	(1 Tbs)
75 mL granulated sugar	(⅓ cup)
250 mL blanched whole almonds	(1 cup)
2 mL vanilla	(½ tsp)
1 mL salt	(¼ tsp)

Spread a 40 cm (16") strip of aluminum foil on a baking sheet.

Combine the butter, corn syrup and sugar in a heavy skillet. Bring the mixture to a boil over medium heat, stirring constantly. Add the almonds and cook, stirring almost constantly for about 10 minutes, until the almonds are golden brown. Stir in the vanilla.

Spread the nut mixture in a single layer on the foil. Sprinkle with salt. Cool and break into clusters of 2 or 3 nuts.
Yields 375 mL (1½ cups) glazed almonds.

Variation:

Glazed Nuts

Substitute pecans, walnuts, peanuts, or a combination of these, for the almonds.

SPICED NUTS

250 mL blanched whole almonds	(1 cup)
125 mL pecan halves	(½ cup)
500 mL walnut halves	(2 cups)
2 egg whites pinch of salt	
250 mL granulated sugar	(1 cup)
5 mL cinnamon	(1 tsp)
1 mL freshly grated nutmeg	(¼ tsp)
1 mL ground allspice	(¼ tsp)
125 mL butter	(½ cup)
2 mL salt	(½ tsp)

Preheat the oven to 150°C (300°F).

Place all of the nuts in a single layer on a baking sheet and toast for about 10 minutes, or until light brown.

Meanwhile, beat the egg whites and the pinch of salt until they form soft peaks. Gradually add the sugar and beat until stiff. Add the spices. Fold the toasted nuts into the egg white mixture.

Melt the butter on a large baking sheet that has 2.5 cm (1") sides. Spread the nut mixture on the sheet and sprinkle with salt. Bake for about 30 minutes, stirring often, until the nuts are brown and no butter remains. Spread out on foil and cool.
Yields about 2 L (8 cups) nuts.

CANDIED CITRUS PEEL

Candied peel is an elegant accompaniment to after-dinner coffee and liqueur and a flavourful change from commercial peel in cakes and breads.

2 large oranges and 1 grapefruit **or**	
4 oranges or a combination of fruits	
175 mL water	(¾ cup)
425 mL granulated sugar additional granulated sugar	(1¾ cups)

With a very fine grater, lightly smooth the outer surface of the fruit. Do not remove much of the colour. Remove the peel from the fruit in quarters with a sharp knife. Place the peel in a saucepan, cover with cold water and soak for 1 hour.

Drain the peel, cover it again with cold water and bring slowly to a boil. Drain again and repeat the process. Cover again with cold water, bring slowly to a boil, then simmer, covered, for 20 minutes, or until the rind is very tender. Drain.

Scrape the inside of the rind to remove any of the bitter white substance. Cut into 6 mm (¼") strips with scissors.

Bring the 175 mL water and the 425 mL granulated sugar to a boil. Add the peel and cook gently for 20 minutes, uncovered, until it has absorbed most of the syrup and the peel is translucent. Cool in the syrup.

Reheat gently, just so the peel can be lifted out of the syrup. Separate the strips and place on wax paper. Put a small amount of granulated sugar in a bag and shake the peel in it, a few strips at a time. Let the peel dry in the air for an hour or longer.

The candied peel will keep indefinitely if stored in an air-tight container and will actually improve in taste after 2 to 3 weeks. Yields about 500 mL (2 cups) peel.

Variation:

Chocolate-Orange Peel

For a delicious variation, dip the candied orange peel in melted semi-sweet chocolate or in the Fondant dip from page 70, instead of rolling it in granulated sugar.

POPCORN BALLS

Long strings of popcorn adorned the branches of Victorian Christmas trees. It's fun to use this decoration today, too, but don't forget to make some extra popcorn balls for the children.

375	mL firmly packed brown sugar	(1½ cups)
125	mL corn syrup	(½ cup)
30	mL water	(2 Tbs)
50	mL vinegar	(¼ cup)
1	mL salt	(¼ tsp)
30	mL butter	(2 Tbs)
5	mL vanilla	(1 tsp)
2	L freshly made popcorn	(8 cups)

Mix the first six ingredients together in a large heavy saucepan. Stir over medium heat until the mixture comes to a boil. Then cook, without stirring, until the mixture reaches the hard ball stage (125°C or 260°F). Remove from the heat and add the vanilla. Pour immediately over the popcorn and mix quickly, making sure to coat all of the kernels.

Wet your hands with cold water and press a small quantity of coated popcorn into a firm ball. Place on wax paper to cool. Yields ten 5 cm (2") balls.

Variation:

Rice-Nut Balls

Substitute 1.25 L (5 cups) puffed rice cereal and 175 mL (¾ cup) coarsely chopped peanuts for the popcorn. Proceed as for Popcorn Balls.

CHOCOLATES

(Uncooked Fondant)

There is very little difference between the taste of this uncooked fondant and the cooked kind, which must be wrestled with for several hours. Uncooked fondant is also easier to roll around interesting centres, and it is something your children can easily handle.

125	mL butter	(½ cup)
2.75	L icing sugar	(11 cups)
325	mL sweetened condensed milk	(1⅓ cups)
45	mL corn syrup	(3 Tbs)
8	squares unsweetened chocolate	(8 oz)
2	cm cube paraffin wax food colouring and flavouring	(1″)

Cream the butter thoroughly. Gradually mix in the icing sugar. Stir in the milk and corn syrup and mix until well combined. Turn out onto a board that has been lightly dusted with icing sugar and knead until smooth.

Divide the fondant into a number of small bowls and add colour as desired. Roll the fondant around one of the centres suggested at the end of this recipe, adding flavouring as indicated.

Let the finished centres sit for a few minutes in the air before you dip them, or make them one day, store in a container and dip the next day.

To make the dip, melt the chocolate and wax in the top of a double boiler. Keep the water hot, but not boiling while you dip the centres.

Have handy a chilled baking sheet covered with wax paper.

Using a small metal knitting needle, spear each centre and quickly dip into melted chocolate, rolling to cover the whole surface. Let it drip well to remove excess chocolate, then place on wax paper to harden.

If you have any melted chocolate left over, try dipping candied peel, brandied cherries, bite-sized pieces of crystallized ginger or whole nuts to add variety to your chocolate box.

Store in a cool, dark place. Serve each chocolate in miniature crinkled paper cups. Yields about 2 kg (4 lbs) fondant.

Suggestions for Centres

Almond flavouring and candied cherries.
Vanilla flavouring and well-drained maraschino cherries soaked in brandy and well drained again.
Maple flavouring and walnut halves.
Vanilla flavouring and candied ginger.
Orange flavouring and orange peel.
Lemon flavouring and lemon peel.
Orange flavouring and pecan halves.
Rum to taste and peanuts.
Melted chocolate and instant coffee powder to taste.
Melted chocolate and peppermint flavouring.
Green colouring and peppermint flavouring.
Vanilla flavouring and whole filberts, brazil nuts or whole almonds.

A CUP OF CHEER

INTRODUCTION

Eggnogs and assorted punches have always been popular for holiday entertaining. This 1853 recipe for Rum Punch shows the simple origins of today's exotic Christmas drinks (the ingredients in parentheses were not included in the original recipe):

> One sour (lemon)
> Two sweet (sugar)
> Four strong (rum)
> Eight weak (water)

The recipes which follow reflect the sophisticated, yet easy-to-make holiday drinks now popular in Canadian homes.

TRADITIONAL HOLIDAY EGGNOG

6 eggs, separated	
1 mL salt	(¼ tsp)
150 mL powdered fruit sugar	(⅔ cup)
625 mL light cream	(2½ cups)
250 mL milk	(1 cup)
250 mL rum or brandy	(1 cup)
300 mL heavy cream	(1¼ cups)
freshly grated nutmeg	

Beat the egg whites and salt together until frothy. Gradually beat in half the sugar and continue beating until stiff peaks form.

Beat the egg yolks until light. Gradually add the remaining sugar, beating until thick and lemon-coloured.

Beating constantly, very slowly add the light cream, milk and spirit to the egg yolk mixture.

Whip the heavy cream until soft peaks form. Fold the whipped cream and stiff egg whites into the egg yolk and cream mixture.

Chill thoroughly. Sprinkle with nutmeg before serving.

Yields about 12 servings.

CITRUS-RUM PUNCH

125 mL granulated sugar	(½ cup)
50 mL boiling water	(¼ cup)
175 mL frozen lemonade concentrate	(¾ cup)
175 mL frozen orange juice concentrate	(¾ cup)
250 mL grapefruit juice	(1 cup)
5 mL orange bitters	(1 tsp)
750 mL golden rum	(3 cups)
1.25 L soda water	(5 cups)
lemon and orange slices	

Dissolve the sugar in boiling water. Cool.

Combine the lemonade and orange juice concentrates, grapefruit juice, orange bitters and rum. Mix well. Add the sugar syrup.

Just before serving, pour the punch mixture over a block of ice in a punch bowl and add soda water. (Blocks of ice can be made by freezing water in milk cartons or plastic containers.) Stir well. Garnish with lemon and orange slices.

Yields 26 servings.

WHITE WINE-BRANDY PUNCH

250	mL winter fruit (see method)	(1 cup)
250	mL brandy	(1 cup)
2.25	L chilled sauterne	(9 cups)
750	mL chilled soda water	(3 cups)

Choose a combination of peeled orange or grapefruit segments, lemon slices or fresh pineapple chunks. Place 250 mL of fruit in a punch bowl, add the brandy, cover and refrigerate overnight.

Just before serving, place a large block of ice in the punch bowl and pour in the sauterne and soda water.
Yields 30 servings.

SAUTERNE-FRUIT PUNCH

This is a very light, pleasant punch that goes a long way.

	red and green maraschino cherries	
2.5	L sauterne	(10 cups)
1.5	L unsweetened orange juice	(6 cups)
1.5	L unsweetened pineapple juice	(6 cups)
175	mL frozen lemonade concentrate	(¾ cup)
750	mL soda water or ginger ale	(3 cups)

Rinse the excess colour from the red and green cherries. Alternating the colours, arrange the cherries in the bottom of a ring mould. Pour in just enough cold water to cover the cherries. Freeze until solid. Add enough cold water to fill the mould and freeze again.

Combine the sauterne, orange and pineapple juice and lemonade concentrate in a chilled punch bowl.

Just before serving, add the soda water. Unmould the maraschino ice ring by dipping it quickly into hot water. Add to the punch. Yields 50 servings.

CRANBERRY PUNCH

This colourful punch is refreshing and not overly sweet.

1	seedless orange	
175	mL frozen lemonade concentrate	(¾ cup)
375	mL frozen orange juice concentrate	(1½ cup)
1.5	L cranberry cocktail	(6 cups)
750	mL gin (optional)	(3 cups)
750	mL soda water	(3 cups)

Thinly slice the orange and place the slices around the bottom of a ring mould. Pour in just enough water to cover the slices and freeze until solid. Add enough cold water to fill mould and freeze again.

Combine the lemonade and orange juice concentrates, cranberry cocktail and gin in a chilled punch bowl.

Just before serving, add the soda water. Unmould the orange ice ring by dipping it quickly into hot water. Add to the punch. Yields 40 servings.

WASSAIL BOWL

The custom of preparing a Wassail Bowl at Christmas was borrowed from the Saxons who drank from it to the toast of "Waes Hael"–"Good Health." It was the traditional English "cup of cheer," and British settlers were quick to introduce it to Canada.

3	small apples	
7.5	cm piece cinnamon stick	(3")
5	cm piece dried ginger root	(2")
4	coriander seeds	
3	whole cloves	
3	whole allspice berries	
2	cardamom seeds	
250	mL water	(1 cup)
250	mL granulated sugar	(1 cup)
2	mL freshly grated nutmeg	(½ tsp)
1	mL mace	(¼ tsp)
1.125	L ale	(4½ cups)
750	mL dry sherry or madeira	(3 cups)
3	eggs, separated	

Wash, core and bake the apples at 180°C (350°F) for 30 to 45 minutes, or until tender, but not mushy.

Tie all of the whole spices together in a cheesecloth bag. Combine the water and sugar in a large pot. Add the spice bag, grated nutmeg and mace. Bring to a boil, stirring until sugar is dissolved. Reduce the heat and simmer for 10 minutes. Add the ale and sherry. Heat to just below the boiling point.

Meanwhile, beat the egg whites until stiff and beat the egg yolks until thick. Fold the whites into the yolks in a heatproof punch bowl.

Remove the spice bag and add the heated liquid very gradually to the eggs, stirring briskly after each addition. Float the roasted apples on top. Serve hot. Yields 12 servings.

MULLED WINE

1	lemon	
150	mL powdered fruit sugar	(⅔ cup)
250	mL water	(1 cup)
5	mL whole cloves	(1 tsp)
7.5	cm piece cinnamon stick	(3")
1	mL freshly grated nutmeg	(¼ tsp)
1.25	L dry red wine, preferably Burgundy	(5 cups)
10	twists of lemon peel	

Slice the unpeeled lemon thinly and place in a saucepan. Add the sugar, water and spices. Stir over medium heat until the sugar is dissolved and the mixture boils. Simmer for 10 minutes, stirring occasionally.

Pour the wine into a large saucepan. Strain the sugar syrup into wine, discarding the spices and lemon slices. Heat the syrup and wine gently to the simmering point. Serve hot with twists of lemon peel as a garnish. Yields 10 servings.

Variation:

Spicy Wine Punch

To serve cold, strain the syrup into a pitcher, rather than a saucepan. Add the wine and chill. Just before serving, add 250 mL (1 cup) chilled ginger ale or soda water. Garnish with twists of lemon peel.
Yields 12 servings.

MULLED CIDER

1.25 L cider	(5 cups)
50 mL lemon juice	(¼ cup)
50 mL lightly packed brown sugar	(¼ cup)
4 whole cloves	
4 cm piece cinnamon stick	(1½")
4 cm piece dry ginger root	(1½")
freshly grated nutmeg	

Combine the cider, lemon juice and brown sugar in a stainless steel pot. Heat the mixture slowly to the simmering point.

Meanwhile, tie the cloves, cinnamon stick and ginger root together in a piece of cheesecloth. Add the bag of spices to the simmering liquid and heat over low heat for 15 minutes. Remove the spice bag. (You may prepare the mulled cider to this point and reheat slowly later.)

Serve hot with a sprinkling of nutmeg in mugs.
Yields 6 servings.

Variation:

Old Stone Fence

Add 50 mL (3 Tbs) rum to each mug of Mulled Cider.

IRISH COFFEE

The holidays are a good excuse for this popular coffee.

powdered fruit sugar	
5 mL granulated sugar	(1 tsp)
50 mL Irish whiskey	(¼ cup)
150 mL very hot strong black coffee	(⅔ cups)
15 mL whipped cream	(1 Tbs)

Rinse a 250 mL (8 oz) stemmed goblet with very hot water. Invert and shake, then dip the rim in a dish of powdered fruit sugar.

Place the granulated sugar in the glass, leave in the spoon and pour in the Irish whisky and coffee. Stir to dissolve the sugar and serve hot topped with whipped cream. Yields 1 serving.

RUDI'S EGG LIQUEUR

This Christmas liqueur was named after the man who shared the recipe with the Canadian Home Economics Association for publications in *The Laura Secord Canadian Cook Book.*

10 egg yolks	
1 envelope vanilla sugar	
1.25 L milk	(5 cups)
550 mL granulated sugar	(2¼ cups)
375-500 mL alcool (available at liquor stores)	(1½-2 cups)

Beat together the egg yolks and vanilla sugar.

Mix the milk and sugar together in a saucepan. Bring to a boil, stirring constantly until sugar is dissolved. Remove from the heat. Stir some of the hot milk into the beaten egg yolks and then gradually stir the egg yolks into the hot mixture.

Reheat over medium heat, stirring constantly, until the first bubbles appear. Do not boil: this will cause the mixture to curdle.

Cool the custard mixture. Thoroughly blend in the alcool. Pour into sterilized bottles. Seal tightly and store on sides in a cool dark place. Age for 2 weeks before using. It will keep indefinitely.
Yields about 1.5 L (3 pints).

HOLIDAY FEASTS

INTRODUCTION

The following are suggested menus for those special holiday meals. The recipes for the soups, meat, poultry, garnishes and vegetables appear in this chapter along with additional recipes that have not been included in the menus. All the breads, desserts, drinks and candies can be found in their appropriate chapters.

Réveillon, a French-Canadian Christmas Eve Supper

Tourtière
Tangy Cabbage Salad   Zesty Baked Beans
Ragoût de Boulettes
Assorted pickles and relishes
Dinner Rolls   Butter
Bûche de Noel (Yule Log)

Traditional Christmas Dinner

Mushroom Consommé
Roast Goose with Onion-Sage Dressing
Giblet Gravy
Spiced Apples
Whipped Potato Casserole
Red Cabbage with Apple
Ginger-Glazed Carrots or Fiddleheads
Steamed Carrot Pudding
Fluffy White Pudding Sauce
Spiced Nuts   Coffee
Candied Citrus Peel

Christmas Dinner from Earlier Times

Traditional Holiday Eggnog
Maple-Glazed Stuffed Pork
Baked Cranberry Sauce
Rice-Mushroom Ring with
Buttered Green Peas
Turnip Puff
Pumpkin-Mincemeat Pie with
Whipped cream
Coffee

Holiday Brunch

Winter Fruit Salad with Cream Dressing
Creamy Scrambled Eggs
Glazed Canadian Back Bacon
Butter Kringle
Coffee   Rudi's Egg Liqueur

New Year's Dinner

Mulled Wine
Potted Cheese   Herb Batter Bread
Roast Duck with Rice and Apricot Dressing
Pan Gravy
Tangy Cranberry Relish
Breaded Parsnips
Lemony Brussels Sprouts
Steamed Fig Pudding
Foamy Orange Sauce
Irish Coffee

Open House

Cranberry Punch
Potted Cheese and Crackers
Spiced Beef   Pickled Mushrooms
Scalloped Oysters   Herb Batter Bread
Butter
Assorted Cookies and Christmas Cakes
Coffee

CLAM CHOWDER

This Clam Chowder from Nova Scotia makes an interesting focal point for a tree-trimming party.

125	mL diced salt pork	(½ cup)
1	large onion, minced	
250	mL diced celery	(1 cup)
250	mL peeled diced raw potatoes	(1 cup)
250	mL diced carrots	(1 cup)
540	mL can of tomatoes	(19 oz)
284	g can of clams	(10 oz)
7	mL salt (or to taste)	(1½ tsp)
1	mL dried crushed thyme	(¼ tsp)

Melt the salt pork in a saucepan over low heat until crisp and brown. Add the vegetables and stir together for 5 to 8 minutes. Add the tomatoes, the liquid drained from the clams, salt and thyme. Bring to a boil. Cover and simmer over low heat for 30 minutes.

Add the clams, heat through and serve immediately. Do not boil the clams.

Serve the chowder with a jug of cold rich cream so that each person can add it to taste. Yields 6 servings.

MUSHROOM CONSOMMÉ

A delicate beginning for a holiday meal.

30	mL butter	(2 Tbs)
30	mL minced green onion	(2 Tbs)
700	g mushrooms	(1½ lbs)
1.5	L homemade beef stock or canned consommé (see note)	(6 cups)
	salt if needed	
250	mL dry sherry	(1 cup)
5	mL lemon juice	(1 tsp)
1	lemon, thinly sliced	

Heat the butter in a large saucepan and sauté the green onion for about 3 minutes, or until translucent.

Grind the mushrooms in a food grinder or food processor fitted with a steel blade. Add to the cooking onion. Cook for 5 minutes, stirring often.

Stir in the broth and bring to a boil. Reduce the heat and simmer, uncovered, for 30 minutes. Cool.

Strain, but allow some bits of mushroom into the consommé. Season with salt if necessary. Add the sherry and lemon juice. Reheat slowly to the simmering point just before serving. Garnish each serving with a thin slice of lemon.
Yields 6 to 8 servings.

Note: If you use canned consommé, dilute according to the instructions on the can before adding.

ROAST GOOSE WITH ONION-SAGE DRESSING

Geese were useful additions to pioneer farms. Their down provided warm quilts for cold winter nights; their feathers and wings made excellent dusters; their eggs were worth four hens' eggs; and they provided a beautiful Christmas dinner long before people raised and ate turkey. Although very rich, a goose cooked properly and grease-free is a treat not to be overlooked.

5	kg goose	(10 lbs)
50	mL seedless raisins	(¼ cup)
125	mL dry red wine	(½ cup)
125	mL butter	(½ cup)
500	mL minced onion	(2 cups)
1	large tart apple, peeled, cored and minced	
250	mL minced celery with leaves	(1 cup)
125	mL coarsely chopped pecans	(½ cup)
1.5	L fresh bread crumbs	(6 cups)
5	mL granulated sugar	(1 tsp)
2	mL salt	(½ tsp)
2	mL freshly ground black pepper	(½ tsp)
5	mL sage	(1 tsp)
2	mL savory	(½ tsp)
	lemon juice	
	salt and pepper	
1	L boiling water or stock	(4 cups)

Remove any loose fat from the goose. Wipe off and dry thoroughly inside and out. Reserve the neck, wing tips, gizzard, heart and liver for the stock and dressing. Chop the liver.

To prepare the dressing, combine the raisins with the red wine. Bring to a boil and boil for 3 minutes. Remove from the heat and cool. Drain the raisins and reserve the wine.

Melt the butter, add the onion, apple and goose liver and sauté until the onion is translucent and the liver loses its pinkness. Add the celery and mix well. Remove from the heat and stir in the pecans and cooked raisins.

In a large bowl, combine the bread crumbs, sugar, salt, pepper and other spices. Add the onion-liver mixture and combine thoroughly. Cool.

Preheat the oven to 200°C (400°F). Rub the goose inside and out with lemon juice and sprinkle the inside with salt and pepper.

Stuff the neck cavity loosely with some of the dressing and fasten the neck skin to the body with a skewer. Stuff the body cavity loosely with the rest of the dressing. Tie or sew shut. Tie the legs close to the body. Using a needle, prick the skin all over to allow the fat to escape.

Put the goose, breast side down, on rack in shallow roasting pan. Pour 500 mL (2 cups) boiling water or stock over it. (Pouring boiling water over the goose and roasting it will help remove the excess fat.) Roast at 200°C (400°F) for 20 minutes, uncovered. Reduce the heat to 160°C (325°F) and roast for 1 hour. Pour off the liquid and baste with the reserved wine. (Keep the wine warm for basting as the goose continues to cook.)

Turn the goose on one side and pour over it 500 mL (2 cups) boiling water. Roast for 30 minutes. Pour off the liquid and baste. Turn on the other side and roast for 30 minutes. Prick the goose again, pour off the drippings and baste. Roast on its back for 1½ hours more, or until tender. The inside temperature should reach 90°C (190°F). The roasting time will be about 3½ to 4 hours in all.

Remove the roast goose from the oven and let it rest for 15 minutes in a warm place so that the juices will be sealed in. Remove the dressing and keep the goose warm for carving. Serve hot with Spiced Apples. Yields 8 servings.

GIBLET GRAVY
Stock

	giblets (neck, wing tips, gizzard and heart from goose or turkey)	
	cold water	
1	small onion, coarsely chopped	
1	stalk celery with leaves	
1	large sprig parsley	
1	carrot, coarsely chopped	
4	peppercorns	
2	mL salt	(½ tsp)
2	mL thyme leaves	(½ tsp)

Gravy

750	mL giblet stock	(3 cups)
30	mL cornstarch	(2 Tbs)
50	mL cold water	(¼ cup)
	salt and pepper to taste	

To make the stock, put the giblets in a saucepan and just cover with cold water. Bring to a boil and skim off any foam. Add the vegetables and spices. Bring to a boil again. Reduce the heat, cover and simmer for about 2 hours. Remove the giblets and reserve. Strain the liquid, discarding the vegetables and peppercorns. Chop the giblets and reserve in the refrigerator.

To make the gravy, remove any excess fat from drippings left in the roast pan after the bird is done. Pour the giblet stock into the pan with the remaining drippings and heat, stirring the brown bits from the pan.

Dissolve the cornstarch in cold water and add, stirring constantly. Simmer the gravy for about 5 minutes, or until smooth and thick. To thicken the gravy, dissolve more cornstarch and add to the gravy; to thin the gravy gradually stir in more hot stock or hot water.

Taste for seasoning and add salt and pepper to taste. Stir in the cooked giblets and heat through. Serve in a warm gravy boat. Yields 8 servings.

SPICED APPLES

Delicious on their own, these spiced apples also make a superb garnish for roast goose. Place a dab of red currant jelly in the middle of each and arrange around the goose.

4	large tart apples	
30	mL lemon juice	(2 Tbs)
750	mL water	(3 cups)
375	mL granulated sugar	(1½ cups)
15	mL lemon juice	(1 Tbs)
	cinnamon	

Preheat the oven to 190°C (375°F).

Peel, halve and core the apples. Sprinkle immediately with the 30 mL of lemon juice.

In a large skillet, combine the water, sugar and the remaining lemon juice and simmer for 5 minutes, uncovered. Add the apple halves and poach them over medium heat for about 10 minutes, or until barely tender, but not soft. Turn them once as they poach.

Remove the apple halves with a slotted spoon and arrange, cut side down, in a baking dish. Sprinkle with cinnamon.

Over high heat, reduce the syrup in the skillet to 125 mL (½ cup). Pour the syrup over the apples and bake for about 15 minutes, basting with syrup once, and turning once as the apples cook. Yields 8 apple halves.

ROAST TURKEY
WITH SAUSAGE DRESSING

Turkey became a popular Christmas meat as early as the nineteenth century in Canada. Today, it is often served throughout the rest of the year as well.

If you can't find a fresh turkey, thaw the frozen bird in the refrigerator. (It might take 3 or 4 days to thaw a 12 kg [24 lb] turkey.) The turkey should be roasted as soon as it has been stuffed and dressed and basted often because the meat is drier than goose or duck.

As new breeds of turkey are developed, the roasting time is decreasing. Don't be surprised if your bird is done before the time you have allowed it. Normally, the turkey should take about 20 minutes per 0.5 kg or pound.

6-7	kg turkey (see note)	(12-15 lbs)
500	g bulk sausage meat	(1 lb)
125	mL chopped onion	(½ cup)
125	mL diced celery	(½ cup)
50	mL minced parsley	(¼ cup)
2	L cubed day-old bread	(8 cups)
5	mL granulated sugar	(1 tsp)
5	mL dried crushed sage	(1 tsp)
5	mL salt	(1 tsp)
2	mL freshly ground black pepper	(½ tsp)
	salt and pepper	
125	mL soft butter	(½ cup)

Wipe off the turkey and dry it thoroughly inside and out. Reserve the neck and giblets for stock.

To prepare the dressing, sauté the sausage meat in a heavy skillet, stirring frequently, until no sign of pink remains. Add the onion, celery and parsley and sauté until the onion is translucent. Drain the excess grease from the pan and set the mixture aside to cool.

Place the bread cubes in a large bowl and mix in the sugar, sage, salt and pepper. Add the sausage and vegetable mixture and combine well.

Preheat the oven to 230°C (450°F).

Sprinkle the inside of the turkey with salt and pepper.

Stuff the neck cavity loosely with some of the dressing and fasten the neck skin to the body with a skewer. Stuff the body cavity loosely with the rest of the dressing and tie or sew shut. Tie the legs and wings close to the body.

Spread half of the soft butter over the breast side of the bird and cover the breast with a double thickness of cheesecloth. Place the turkey, breast side down on rack in a shallow roasting pan. Spread the rest of the butter over the back of the turkey.

Roast for 20 minutes at 230°C (450°F). Reduce the heat to 160°C (325°F) and continue roasting until the internal temperature of the bird is 90°C (190°F), or until the juices run clear when you insert a skewer in the thickest part of the thigh. Turn the turkey onto its back halfway through the roasting time and remove the cheesecloth carefully 1 hour before it is done. Baste the turkey with the pan juices often throughout the roasting time.

Let the roasted turkey rest 15 minutes in a warm place so that the juices will be sealed in. Remove the dressing before carving. Serve with Giblet Gravy (page 79) and Baked Cranberry Sauce (page 81) or Tangy Cranberry Relish (page 81).
Yields about 20 servings.

Note: Although there are pre-basted turkeys on the market, it is much more economical to baste the turkey with butter yourself as it roasts. The sausage meat will add moisture to the meat as well.

BAKED CRANBERRY SAUCE

Delicious with roast turkey, pork, goose and duck.

500 mL fresh cranberries	(2 cups)
250 mL lightly packed brown sugar	(1 cup)
1 mL ground cloves	(¼ tsp)

Preheat the oven to 180°C (350°F).

Wash the cranberries and place them in a 1 L (1 quart) baking dish. Sprinkle the brown sugar and cloves over them. Cover and bake for 30 minutes, stirring occasionally.
Yields 325 mL (1⅓ cups) cranberries.

TANGY CRANBERRY RELISH

This uncooked relish is good with roast turkey and pork.

500 mL fresh cranberries	(2 cups)
1 orange	
½ lemon	
250 mL granulated sugar	(1 cup)
125 mL seedless raisins	(½ cup)
125 mL chopped walnuts	(½ cup)
5 mL ground cloves	(1 tsp)

Grind the cranberries in a meat grinder or food processor fitted with a steel blade.

Remove the thin outer rind (zest) from the orange and lemon and reserve. Peel off the white pith and discard. Cut the orange and lemon into sections. Remove the seeds.

Grind the rind and fruit and add to the cranberries. Add the sugar and stir well to dissolve. Thoroughly mix in the remaining ingredients.

Refrigerate overnight so that the flavours will mingle. The relish will keep for about a week in the refrigerator and freezes well, too.
Yields about 875 mL (3½ cups) relish.

BRANDIED CRANBERRIES

Serve with roast turkey, duck or goose.

375 mL granulated sugar	(1½ cups)
50 mL brandy	(¼ cup)
125 mL water	(½ cup)
125 mL orange juice	(½ cup)
35 mL grated orange rind	(2¼ Tbs)
1 L fresh cranberries	(4 cups)
30 mL red currant jelly	(2 Tbs)
5 mL ground ginger	(1 tsp)

Combine the sugar, brandy, water, orange juice and rind in a large heavy saucepan. Bring to a boil, stirring until the sugar is dissolved. Add the cranberries and bring to a boil. Continue boiling, stirring constantly, for about 5 minutes, or until the skins pop.

Remove from the heat and add the currant jelly and ginger. Mix well and refrigerate. Serve cold.
Yields about 1 L (4 cups) cranberries.

ROAST DUCK WITH RICE AND APRICOT DRESSING

Browning the duck before stuffing it eliminates much of the grease that might otherwise be absorbed by the dressing.

2	kg duck	(5 lbs)
	salt and freshly ground black pepper	
50	mL butter	(¼ cup)
50	mL chopped celery	(¼ cup)
50	mL chopped onion	(¼ cup)
150	mL brown rice	(⅔ cup)
125	mL sliced mushrooms	(½ cup)
2	mL salt	(½ tsp)
2	mL m.s.g.	(½ tsp)
2	mL ground savory	(½ tsp)
1	mL freshly ground black pepper	(¼ tsp)
375	mL chicken stock	(1½ cups)
250	mL diced dried apricots	(1 cup)
50	mL chopped pecans	(¼ cup)
125	mL chicken stock	(½ cup)
125	mL dry white wine	(½ cup)
10	mL cornstarch	(2 tsp)
30	mL cold water	(2 Tbs)
	canned apricot slices, drained	
	watercress	

Preheat the oven to 230°C (450°F).

Wipe off the duck and dry it thoroughly inside and out. Rub the skin with salt and pepper. Place on a rack in a shallow pan. Using a needle, prick the skin all over to allow the fat to escape.

Roast at 230°C (450°F) for 30 minutes, uncovered, until the skin is well browned. Transfer the duck to a large oven-proof casserole and set aside while preparing the stuffing. Pour the fat out of the shallow roasting pan, keeping any brown bits in the pan. Put the pan to one side until the duck is stuffed. Reduce the oven temperature to 160°C (325°F).

To make the stuffing, melt the butter in a large frying pan. Add the celery and onion and sauté until translucent. Add the brown rice, mushrooms and seasonings and cook, stirring occasionally, over low heat until the rice starts to brown. Add enough stock to just cover the rice in the pan. Add the dried apricots. Cover and simmer for 35 to 40 minutes. If, at the end of this time, there is still liquid in the pan, remove the lid and continue cooking until it is all absorbed. Remove from the heat. Add the pecans and cool.

Stuff the browned duck loosely with the rice mixture. Truss and tie securely. Add the 125 mL chicken stock and the wine to the browning pan. Bring to a boil, scrape up all the brown bits and pour over the duck. Cover the casserole and roast at 160°C (325°F) for 1½ hours, or until the temperature of the thickest part of the thigh reaches 82-88°C (180-190°F). Transfer the cooked duck to a hot platter and keep warm.

To make the sauce, skim off as much fat as possible from the casserole. Dissolve the cornstarch in the cold water and stir gradually into the pan drippings. Reduce the heat and simmer for 5 minutes.

Surround the duck with apricot slices, garnish with watercress and serve hot with the sauce.

Yields 4 servings.

MAPLE-GLAZED STUFFED PORK

2	kg centre-cut pork loin roast and tenderloin end	(4-5 lbs)
50	mL butter	(¼ cup)
125	mL chopped onion	(½ cup)
250	mL chopped celery	(1 cup)
250	mL finely diced mushrooms	(1 cup)
5	mL salt	(1 tsp)
2	mL grated orange rind	(½ tsp)
2	mL dried crushed basil	(½ tsp)
1	mL dried crushed thyme	(¼ tsp)
1	mL powdered or ground sage	(¼ tsp)
50	mL chopped parsley	(¼ cup)
1	mL freshly ground black pepper	(¼ tsp)
250	mL dry bread crumbs	(1 cup)
125	mL maple syrup	(½ cup)
125	mL orange juice	(½ cup)
	orange	
	fresh parsley	

Remove the ribs from roast and flatten the tenderloin portion as much as possible.

Melt the butter in a large skillet. Add the vegetables and sauté until the onion is translucent. Remove from the heat. Stir in the salt, orange rind, herbs, pepper and bread crumbs.

Preheat the oven to 220°C (425°F). Fill the roast with the stuffing, place the tenderloin portion on top and tie tightly. Place on a rack in a shallow pan and roast at 220°C for 20 minutes. Reduce the heat to 160°C (325°F) and roast for about 3 more hours, or until a meat thermometer registers an inside temperature of 80°C (170°F).

Meanwhile, combine the maple syrup and orange juice, and during the last hour of roasting, baste the pork with the mixture every 15 minutes.

Slice the orange thinly and place in roasting pan 30 minutes before the meat is done. Serve the pork garnished with the orange slices and lots of fresh parsley. Yields 8 servings.

GLAZED CANADIAN BACK BACON

Glazed Back Bacon provides a delicious focus for a holiday brunch.

1	kg centre-cut peameal back bacon	(2 lbs)
125	mL brown sugar	(½ cup)
30	mL all-purpose flour	(2 Tbs)
2	mL dry mustard	(½ tsp)
0.5	mL ground cloves	(⅛ tsp)
125	mL apple cider	(½ cup)
15	mL cider vinegar	(1 Tbs)

Preheat the oven to 160°C (325°F).

Place the bacon in a shallow baking pan. Combine the brown sugar, flour, mustard and cloves. Gradually stir the liquids into the brown sugar mixture. Spread over the bacon.

Bake for 1 hour, basting with the glaze from pan every 15 minutes. Serve hot with Tangy Cranberry Relish (page 81). Yields 8 servings.

HAM COOKED IN BEER

2.5	kg cooked smoked ham	(5 lbs)
	water	
375	mL beer	(1½ cup)
	whole cloves	
125	mL lightly packed brown sugar	(½ cup)
50	mL maple syrup	(¼ cup)
10	mL dry mustard	(2 tsp)
30	mL flour	(2 Tbs)

Place the ham in a large saucepan and pour in water almost to cover. Add the beer and bring to a boil. Reduce the heat to low, partially cover and simmer for 2 hours. Preheat the oven to 180°C (350°F).

Discard the liquid and place the ham on a rack in a shallow baking dish, fat side up. If there is a skin on the ham, remove it. Using a sharp knife, score the fat into diamonds and insert the cloves in the middle of these.

Blend together the brown sugar, maple syrup, dry mustard and flour. Spread this glaze over the ham and cook for 45 minutes. Brush with the pan drippings every 15 minutes. Serve hot or cold, garnished with preserved peach halves and parsley.
Yields 10 to 12 servings.

SPICED BEEF

Wherever the Irish have settled in Canada, Spiced Beef is a favourite, especially at Christmas. It is easy to prepare and keeps for weeks.

12	mL salt	(2½ tsp)
5	mL granulated sugar	(1 tsp)
5	mL salt petre (available in drug stores)	(1 tsp)
45	mL mixed pickling spice	(3 Tbs)
4	dried red pepper chillies	
4	garlic cloves	
1	mL cinnamon	(¼ tsp)
1	mL ground allspice	(¼ tsp)
1	mL mace	(¼ tsp)
2.5	kg boneless round steak roast of beef	(5 lbs)

Place all the ingredients, except the beef, in a blender or food processor and make a fine powder of them, or pound in a mortar. Rub this powder evenly into the meat on all sides. Wrap the roast in heavy foil and place it on a platter in the refrigerator for 10 to 14 days, turning occasionally.

Preheat the oven to 110°C (225°F).

Place the meat in a shallow roasting pan and roast the beef, tightly wrapped in the foil, for 7 hours. Make certain the roast is tightly wrapped throughout the cooking process.

Cool completely in the foil and scrape off most of the outside mixture before slicing the meat into thin slices.
Yields 12 servings.

RAGOÛT DE BOULETTES

4	pork hocks	
	cold water	
6	whole cloves	
1	medium onion	
1	celery stalk with leaves	
1	bay leaf	
10	mL salt	(2 tsp)
	freshly ground black pepper	

Meatballs

700	g ground lean pork	(1½ lbs)
125	mL finely chopped onion	(½ cup)
5	mL salt	(1 tsp)
1	mL dry mustard	(¼ tsp)
1	mL ground cloves	(¼ tsp)
1	mL cinnamon	(¼ tsp)
	freshly ground black pepper	
125	mL dry bread crumbs	(½ cup)
1	egg, beaten	
	flour	
50	mL butter	(¼ cup)
4	medium potatoes, peeled and quartered	
375	mL all-purpose flour	(1½ cups)
	cold water	

Skin the pork hocks, place them in a large pot, and pour in water just to cover. Bring to a boil and skim off any foam that appears on top.

Stick the 6 whole cloves in the onion. Dice the celery. Add the onion, celery, bay leaf, 10 mL salt and the pepper to the pot. Simmer, covered, for 2 hours.

Meanwhile, make the meatballs. Combine the ground pork, chopped onion, 5 mL salt, mustard, cloves, cinnamon, pepper, bread crumbs and egg. Form into small balls. Place in one layer on a baking sheet, cover lightly and refrigerate until the hocks have simmered for 2 hours.

When the hocks have cooked the required time, melt the butter in a heavy skillet, dust the meatballs with flour and brown evenly on all sides. Add them to the pot with the hocks and cook for 15 minutes. Add the potatoes and cook for 30 minutes longer, until the potatoes are tender, but not mushy.

When the pork hocks are tender, remove them from the liquid and cut off the meat in large pieces. Discard the bone and fat. Return the meat to the pot. Discard the bay leaf and whole onion with cloves.

Brown the 375 mL (1½ cups) flour by stirring it in a clean skillet over medium heat until golden. Combine the browned flour and enough cold water to make a smooth runny paste. Gradually add the flour paste to the stock and cook, stirring until there is no starchy taste. This takes about 5 minutes. To thicken the stew, repeat the procedure with a bit more flour. To thin it, slowly stir in a small amount of hot water.

Yields 6 servings.

TOURTIÈRE

This French-Canadian meat pie is traditionally served for Christmas Eve dinner. There is a story that the name originated in the sixteenth century when "tourtes", large wild pigeons, abounded in New France. Settlers felled the birds by the thousands, and thrifty housewives transformed them into a variety of meat pies, including the "tarte à la tourte," now abbreviated to tourtière.

1	medium potato	
500	g ground lean pork	(1 lb)
1	medium chopped onion	
1	stalk celery, cut in three pieces	
1	minced garlic clove	
2	mL salt	(½ tsp)
2	mL powdered sage	(½ tsp)
2	mL dried crushed thyme	(½ tsp)
0.5	mL ground cloves	(⅛ tsp)
	freshly ground black pepper	
	sufficient pastry for a 2-crust 1 L (9") pie (see page 32)	
1	egg, beaten	
15	mL water	(1 Tbs)

Cook the potato in boiling water for 30 minutes, or until tender. Remove with a slotted spoon, mash and set aside. Bring 125 mL (½ cup) of the potato water to a boil and add the pork, vegetables and spices. Simmer, uncovered, over medium heat for about 45 minutes, or until the pork has lost its pink colour and the liquid is reduced by half. Remove the celery. Add the mashed potato and let the mixture cool.

Preheat the oven to 230°C (450°F).

Line a pie pan with pastry. Skim off any excess fat from the surface of the potato and meat mixture and fill the pie shell. Cover with the top pastry, seal and flute the edges. Cut slits in the top pastry to let steam escape. Combine the beaten egg with the water and brush over the top crust.

Bake at 230°C (450°F) for 10 minutes, reduce the heat to 180°C (350°F) and bake for 20 minutes longer, or until the crust is golden.

Serve hot with chili sauce or green tomato pickle.

Tourtières freeze well. Thaw in the refrigerator and reheat, covered with foil, for 20 minutes at 180°C (350°F).
Yields 6 servings.

ACADIAN MEAT PIE

This six-layer meat pie goes by many names —Cipâte, Six-pâtes, Cipaille, Si-paille, Sea-pie, pâté en pâté. And there are just as many recipes for it as names, using a wide range and combination of meat, such as rabbit, venison, moose, partridge or other wild birds, chicken, pork, veal, beef, turkey, lamb, duck and goose.

Filling

1.5	kg chicken	(3 lbs)
1.5	kg rabbit	(3 lbs)
1	kg lean pork	(2 lbs)
1	kg boneless stewing beef	(2 lbs)
2	large onions, chopped	
375	mL diced celery	(1½ cups)
250	mL thinly sliced carrots	(1 cup)
10	mL salt	(2 tsp)
2	mL freshly ground black pepper	(½ tsp)
2	mL ground savoury	(½ tsp)
115	g salt pork	(¼ lb)
750	mL peeled diced potatoes	(3 cups)

Stock

	chicken and rabbit bones	
	cold water	
1	small onion, coarsely chopped	
1	stalk of celery with leaves	
5	mL salt	(1 tsp)
2	mL freshly ground black pepper	(½ tsp)
1	mL dried crushed thyme leaves	(¼ tsp)

Pastry

500	mL all-purpose flour	(2 cups)
5	mL salt	(1 tsp)
7	mL baking powder	(1½ tsp)
150	mL shortening	(⅔ cup)
5	mL white vinegar	(1 tsp)
125	mL milk	(½ cup)
1	egg, lightly beaten	

To make the filling, bone the chicken and rabbit, reserving the bones for stock. Cut the meat into 2 cm (¾") cubes. Cube the pork and beef. Mix together all the meat, onions, celery, carrots, salt, pepper and savory. Cover and refrigerate overnight so that the flavours will mingle.

Meanwhile, prepare the stock. Place chicken and rabbit bones in a saucepan, cover with cold water and bring to a boil. Skim off the foam. Add the onion, celery, salt, pepper and thyme. Simmer, covered, over medium-low heat for 2 hours. Strain and refrigerate the stock until needed. Discard the bones and vegetables.

To prepare the pastry, mix the flour, salt and baking powder together. Using a pastry blender or two knives, cut in the shortening until the mixture resembles coarse rolled oats. Add vinegar and milk and mix in

quickly to make a soft dough. Wrap in wax paper and refrigerate until needed.

When ready to put the pie together, divide the pastry into two parts. On a lightly-floured board, roll out one half to a thickness of 1 cm (⅓"). Cut into 2.5 cm (1") squares. Roll out the other half of the pastry to fit the top of a 3-4 L (3-4 quart) casserole or a dutch oven. (Early versions were baked in black cast-iron pots.)

Preheat the oven to 200°C (400°F).

Finish the filling by rinsing the salt pork thoroughly under cold water to remove the excess salt. Dry it and cut it into strips. Fry the pork strips over medium heat until crisp.

Scatter pork and drippings in bottom of the casserole. Cover with a layer of the meat mixture, then a layer of the diced potatoes and a layer of pastry squares, leaving space between squares. Repeat with the meat, potatoes and pastry squares until everything is used up and the casserole is about three-quarters full. (There is some confusion in old recipes as to whether the six layers meant six layers of pastry or six layers in all. Either way is fine and depends on the shape of your casserole.)

Pour in the reserved stock, to within 5 cm (2") of the top. Cover completely with the full layer of pastry. Seal well to the edge of the casserole. Make a couple of slits in the middle to allow steam to escape and brush with beaten egg.

Bake at 200°C (400°F) for 45 minutes, then reduce the heat to 150°C (300°F) and bake for 4 to 4½ hours longer, or until the meat is tender.

If the pie seems to become too dry while baking, pour in more stock, using a funnel inserted in one of the slits on top.

Serve hot with green tomato relish or chili sauce.

Yields 12 to 14 servings.

SCALLOPED OYSTERS

50	mL butter	(¼ cup)
45	mL chopped green onion	(3 Tbs)
30	mL diced celery	(2 Tbs)
45	mL all-purpose flour	(3 Tbs)
1	mL salt	(¼ tsp)
1	mL freshly ground black pepper	(¼ tsp)
0.5	mL cayenne	(⅛ tsp)
175	mL milk	(¾ cup)
125	mL cream	(½ cup)
375	mL fine cracker crumbs	(1½ cups)
500	mL oysters and their liquid	(1 pint)
	paprika	

Grease a 1.5 L (1½ quart) casserole with butter. Preheat the oven to 200°C (400°F).

Melt the butter and sauté the onion and celery until the onion is translucent. Add the flour, salt, pepper and cayenne. Cook, stirring, for 2 minutes. Remove from the heat. Heat the milk and cream together until lukewarm. Gradually add to the first mixture, stirring constantly. Cook, stirring constantly, until thick.

Place a third of the crumbs in the prepared casserole and cover with half the oysters and liquid and half the vegetable and milk mixture. Cover with another third of the crumbs and repeat the layers, ending with the remainder of the crumbs. There should be no more than two layers of oysters in this dish.

Dust the top with a very light sprinkling of paprika. Bake for 20 to 30 minutes, or until brown.

Yields 6 servings.

CREAMED COD AU GRATIN

Creamed Cod is traditionally served by Maritimers on Boxing Day as a welcome change from the heavy, rich meals of Christmas.

750	g cod fillets	(1½ lbs)
500	mL milk	(2 cups)
45	mL butter	(3 Tbs)
50	mL flour	(¼ cup)
2	mL salt	(½ tsp)
2	mL dry mustard	(½ tsp)
	freshly ground black pepper	
50	mL dry bread crumbs	(¼ cup)
250	mL grated sharp cheddar cheese	(1 cup)

Grease six individual casseroles or one flat 2.5 L (9" x 9") baking dish. Preheat the oven to 180°C (350°F).

Simmer the fish in the milk, covered, for about 10 minutes per 2 cm (1") thickness, or until the fish flakes easily with a fork.

Drain and reserve the milk. Flake the fish into the prepared casseroles.

Melt the butter in the top of a double boiler. Add the flour and cook for 2 to 3 minutes. Remove from the heat and gradually stir in the warm reserved milk. Place back on the heat and cook, stirring, until thick and smooth. Stir in the salt, mustard and black pepper.

Pour the sauce over the fish in the six casseroles. Mix together bread crumbs and cheese and top each casserole with some of this mixture. Place the casseroles in a shallow pan containing 6 mm (¼") hot water. Bake for 25 minutes, or until piping hot and the cheese has melted.

Yields 6 servings.

CREAMY SCRAMBLED EGGS

With the addition of cream cheese, these scrambled eggs will keep longer in a chafing dish for a company brunch.

6	eggs	
50	mL cream	(¼ cup)
50	mL dry white wine	(¼ cup)
2	mL salt	(½ tsp)
	freshly ground black pepper	
30	mL butter	(2 Tbs)
115	g cubed cream cheese	(4 oz)

Beat the eggs lightly. Add the cream, wine, salt and pepper. Melt the butter in a chafing dish or double boiler. Pour in the egg mixture. Stir occasionally over medium-low heat until the eggs are almost firm, but still very moist. Stir in the cream cheese until it melts and blends. Serve hot.
Yields 4 to 6 servings.

ZESTY BAKED BEANS

This dish deserves its name: the dry mustard and pepper give it a real zest. In fact, you may want to cut down on the spices until you've tasted it.

500	mL dried navy beans	(2 cups)
	cold water	
7	mL dry mustard	(½ Tbs)
7	mL freshly ground black pepper	(½ Tbs)
7	mL salt	(½ Tbs)
1	small onion, minced	
100	g diced salt pork	(¼ lb)
125	mL molasses	(½ cup)

Wash and drain the beans and place them in a 2.5 L (2 quart) casserole. Add cold water to cover and soak overnight.

Next morning, preheat the oven to 180°C (350°F). Do not drain the beans. Add the mustard, pepper, salt and onion. Rinse the salt pork in cold water to remove the excess salt before dicing. Stir the diced pork into the beans.

Bake covered for 5 hours. Check often to make sure the beans have not cooked dry. Add more water almost to cover if necessary. Stir occasionally. Half an hour before serving stir in the molasses. Remove the lid for a crusty surface. Yields 6 servings.

WHIPPED POTATO CASSEROLE

It is difficult to prepare potatoes ahead of time, but this delicious casserole provides an easy answer to the problem.

10-12	medium potatoes	
50	mL butter	(¼ cup)
225	g cubed cream cheese	(8 oz)
250	mL sour cream	(1 cup)
	salt and freshly ground pepper	
30	mL melted butter	(2 Tbs)
50	mL dry bread crumbs	(¼ cup)

Grease a 2 L (2 quart) casserole.

Cook the potatoes in boiling salted water in a covered saucepan for 20 to 30 minutes, or until tender. Drain and return to heat briefly to dry.

Mash the potatoes with the butter. Add the cream cheese, sour cream, salt and pepper to taste. Beat until creamy.

Spoon into the prepared casserole. Combine the melted butter with the crumbs and sprinkle evenly on top. Cover tightly and refrigerate until needed.

Preheat the oven to 180°C (350°F).

Remove the casserole from the refrigerator 30 minutes before re-heating. Bake for 20 minutes, or until hot throughout.
Yields 10 servings.

MAPLE-CANDIED SQUASH

1 L	mashed cooked squash	(4 cups)
50 mL	melted butter	(¼ cup)
15 mL	light cream	(1 Tbs)
2 mL	salt	(½ tsp)
	freshly ground black pepper	
	freshly grated nutmeg	
50 mL	chopped pecans or walnuts	(¼ cup)
	30mL maple syrup	(2 Tbs)

Grease a 1.5 L (1½ quart) casserole with butter. Preheat the oven to 180°C (350°F).

Combine the squash, 30 mL (2 Tbs) of the melted butter, cream, salt, pepper and nutmeg. Place in the prepared casserole.

Mix together the rest of the melted butter, nuts and maple syrup. Drizzle over the squash. Bake for 20 minutes, or until a glaze forms on top.
Yields 6 servings.

Variation:

Maple-Candied Sweet Potatoes

Substitute 1 L (4 cups) mashed cooked sweet potatoes for the the squash and proceed as for Maple-Candied Squash.

BUTTERY DICED TURNIP

1 L	peeled diced turnip	(4 cups)
10 mL	brown sugar	(2 tsp)
50 mL	melted butter	(¼ cup)
	salt and freshly ground pepper to taste	

Cover the turnip with boiling water and add the brown sugar. Bring to the boil, then reduce the heat and simmer, covered, for 20 to 25 minutes, or until tender, but not mushy.

Drain, stir in the melted butter and sprinkle with salt and lots of pepper.
Yields 6 servings.

TURNIP PUFF

750 mL	hot mashed turnip (one medium-large turnip)	(3 cups)
30 mL	butter	(2 Tbs)
2	eggs, beaten	
45 mL	all-purpose flour	(3 Tbs)
15 mL	brown sugar	(1 Tbs)
5 mL	baking powder	(1 tsp)
5 mL	salt	(1 tsp)
	freshly ground black pepper	
	freshly grated nutmeg	
15 mL	melted butter	(1 Tbs)
50 mL	dry bread crumbs	(¼ cup)

Grease a 1.5 L (1½ quart) casserole with butter. Preheat the oven to 190°C (375°F).

Combine the turnip, butter and eggs and beat thoroughly. (If you have a food processor, use it to mash the turnip and do the rest of the mixing in it for a fast, smooth dish.) Add the flour, sugar, baking powder, salt, pepper, and nutmeg and mix until well blended. Turn into the prepared casserole. Combine the melted butter and bread crumbs and sprinkle evenly on top. Bake for about 25 minutes until lightly browned.
Yields 6 to 8 servings.

RICE-MUSHROOM RING

This easy-to-make ring is attractive served with bright green vegetables in the centre.

250	mL sliced mushrooms	(1 cup)
50	mL butter	(¼ cup)
125	mL blanched slivered almonds	(½ cup)
30	mL sherry	(2 Tbs)
	freshly grated nutmeg	
625	mL cooked wild rice (see note), white or brown rice	(2½ cups)

Grease a 1 L (4 cup) mould with butter.

Sauté the mushrooms in the butter for 2 to 3 minutes, or until slightly coloured. Stir in the almonds and sherry. Remove from the heat.

Sprinkle nutmeg over the cooked rice and combine the two mixtures. Pack into the mould. (The ring can be refrigerated at this point, if you wish. Bring it back to room temperature before baking.)

Preheat the oven to 180°C (350°F). Set the mould in a shallow pan of hot water and bake for 20 minutes, or until heated through.

To serve, loosen the edges by running a sharp thin knife around the edge. Invert the ring onto a warm platter by placing platter over top, turning over, and carefully removing the ring. Serve hot.
Yields about 6 servings.

Note: To cook the wild rice, wash 150 mL (⅔ cup) raw rice and soak for several hours in cold water. Wash the rice again, changing the water once or twice. Stir the washed rice into 750 mL (3 cups) boiling water, cover, reduce heat to medium-low and cook for 20 minutes, or until tender.

PICKLED MUSHROOMS

Years ago, wild mushrooms were pickled for special winter meals. Today, with mushrooms in common supply, these delicacies are saved for holiday entertaining in Ukrainian-Canadian homes.

500	g small white mushrooms	(1 lb)
375	mL white vinegar	(1½ cups)
375	mL hot water	(1½ cups)
1	bay leaf	
50	mL salad oil	(¼ cup)
10	mL salt	(2 tsp)
5	mL peppercorns	(1 tsp)
1	mL crushed chillies	(¼ tsp)
2	cloves garlic, halved	
2	mL mace	(½ tsp)
150	mL white vinegar (approximately)	(⅔ cup)

Clean the mushrooms and place them in a stainless steel or enamelled saucepan. Cover with the 375 mL white vinegar and hot water. Add the bay leaf. Bring to a boil, reduce the heat and simmer, uncovered, for 5 minutes. Drain and discard the liquid and the bay leaf.

When cool, pack the mushrooms in a jar. Mix together the salad oil, salt, peppercorns, chillies, garlic and mace. Stir until the salt dissolves. Pour the oil and spices over the mushrooms. Pour in enough vinegar to cover (no more than 150 mL). Cover tightly and refrigerate for 2 or 3 days before using. Serve cold and well drained.
Yields about 625 mL (1 pint) mushrooms.

RED CABBAGE WITH APPLE

Canadians of many cultural backgrounds serve red cabbage with roast goose. Since the flavour is enhanced with re-heating, this recipe may be prepared days in advance.

1	kg red cabbage	(2 lbs)
2	medium apples	
50	mL lard	(¼ cup)
125	mL finely chopped onion	(½ cup)
50	mL boiling water	(¼ cup)
50	mL red wine vinegar	(¼ cup)
30	mL granulated sugar	(2 Tbs)
5	mL salt	(1 tsp)
1	small bay leaf	
1	mL ground cloves	(¼ tsp)

Remove the tough outer leaves of the cabbage, quarter and remove the core. Shred the cabbage by hand or in a food processor fitted with a shredding disk. Peel, core and chop the apples.

Heat the lard in a large skillet or saucepan. Add the apples and onions and cook, stirring, for 5 minutes, or until the onion is translucent.

Add the cabbage, water, red wine vinegar, sugar, salt, bay leaf and ground cloves. Bring to a boil, then reduce the heat and cover. Stirring often, cook for about 45 minutes, or until very tender. Check during cooking time to make sure the cabbage is moist. Add a bit more water if needed.

Remove the bay leaf before serving.
Yields 6 servings.

BREADED PARSNIPS

Parsnips are among Canada's sweetest vegetables, but too often they are ignored or improperly cooked. Don't let them become mushy and tasteless with overcooking. Try this delicious version with roast pork.

500	g parsnips	(1 lb)
1	egg	
30	mL milk	(2 Tbs)
2	mL salt	(½ tsp)
	freshly ground black pepper	
1	mL ground or powdered savoury	(¼ tsp)
125	mL dry bread crumbs	(½ cup)
50	mL butter	(¼ cup)

Peel the parsnips and cut them into large pieces about 6 cm (2½″) long. Cook in boiling salted water for 8 to 10 minutes, or until almost tender. Drain.

Beat the egg and milk together. Add the salt, pepper and savoury to the bread crumbs. Melt the butter in a heavy skillet. Dip each piece of parsnip in the egg mixture, then in the crumbs. Cook in the melted butter until golden brown, turning often.
Yields 6 servings.

FIDDLEHEADS

Fiddleheads or ferns are a speciality of New Brunswick, but they are found in other provinces as well. If fresh fiddleheads aren't available, use frozen ones and follow the instructions on the package. Fresh fiddleheads should be cooked for about 8 minutes, or until tender but still crisp. Serve with butter, salt, pepper and lemon juice to taste.

LEMONY BRUSSELS SPROUTS

1	L Brussels sprouts	(4 cups)
500	mL chicken stock	(2 cups)
50	mL butter	(¼ cup)
20	mL lemon juice	(1½ Tbs)
	salt and freshly ground pepper	

Cut the end off each sprout and remove the outer leaves. Soak in ice water for 1 hour. Drain.

Bring the chicken stock to a boil. Add the sprouts and cook, covered, for 12 to 20 minutes, or until just tender, but still bright green. Drain and discard stock.

Meanwhile melt the butter, add the lemon juice and pour over the hot Brussels sprouts. Season with salt and pepper to taste.
Yields 6 servings.

GINGER-GLAZED CARROTS

500	g carrots	(1 lb)
50	mL butter	(¼ cup)
30	mL brown sugar	(2 Tbs)
5	mL ground ginger	(1 tsp)
	salt and freshly ground black pepper	
	minced parsley	

Peel the carrots and cut into matchstick-shaped pieces. In a heavy skillet, melt the butter and add the carrots. Cover with a lid fitted with a buttered round of wax paper. Steam over low heat for 10 to 12 minutes, or until just tender. Remove the lid and paper. Sprinkle the carrots with brown sugar, ginger, salt and pepper. Cook, stirring frequently, for 2 minutes longer, or until glazed. Garnish with a sprinkling of minced parsley.
Yields 6 servings.

TANGY CABBAGE SALAD

Besides making a delicious coleslaw, this recipe is large enough to feed a holiday crowd. It keeps well for at least two weeks. In fact, it is more flavourful if refrigerated for a day before serving.

1	medium cabbage	
250	mL chopped green pepper	(1 cup)
250	mL grated carrot	(1 cup)
1	medium onion, chopped	
15	mL salt	(1 Tbs)
	ice cubes	
125	mL canned pimiento, drained and chopped	(½ cup)

Dressing

250	mL granulated sugar	(1 cup)
175	mL white vinegar	(¾ cup)
125	mL cooking oil	(½ cup)
50	mL water	(¼ cup)
5	mL mustard seed	(1 tsp)
5	mL celery seed	(1 tsp)

Shred the cabbage by hand or in a food processor fitted with a shredding disk. Mix in the green pepper, carrot, onion and salt. Cover with ice cubes and let the mixture crisp for at least 1 hour. Drain well. Add the pimiento.

To make the dressing, boil together the sugar, vinegar, oil, water, mustard and celery seed. Pour the dressing over the cabbage mixture and cool. Turn into a large container, cover and refrigerate.
Yields 12 or more servings.

INDEX